LEVEL E

VOCABULARY

word meaning, pronunciation, prefixes, suffixes, synonyms, antonyms, and fun!

in Action

LOYOLA PRESS.

Chicago

LOYOLA PRESS.

3441 N. Ashland Avenue
Chicago, Illinois 60657
(800) 621-1008
www.loyolapress.com

Cover & Interior Art: Anni Betts
Cover Design: Judine O'Shea
Interior Design: Kathy Greenholdt

Manufactured in the United States of America.

ISBN-10: 0-8294-2773-2

ISBN-13: 978-0-8294-2773-8

15 16 17 Hess 10 9 8 6 7 5 4

Contents

Pronunciation Key

This key shows the meanings of the abbreviations and symbols used throughout the book.

Some English words have more than one possible pronunciation. This book gives only one pronunciation per word, except when different pronunciations indicate different parts of speech. For example, when the word *relay* is used as a noun, it is pronounced rē´ lā; as a verb, the word is pronounced rə lā´.

Parts of Speech

adj.	adjective	*int.*	interjection	*prep.*	preposition
adv.	adverb	*n.*	noun	*part.*	participle
				v.	verb

Vowels

ā	tape	ə	about, circus	ôr	torn
a	map	ī	kite	oi	noise
âr	stare	i	win	ou	foul
ä	car, father	ō	toe	o͞o	soon
ē	meet	o	mop	o͝o	book
e	kept	ô	law	u	tug

Consonants

ch	check	ŋ	rang	y	yellow
g	girl	th	thimble	zh	treasure
j	jam	t̶h̶	that	sh	shelf

Stress

The accent mark follows the syllable receiving the major stress, such as in the word *plaster* (plas´ tər).

Pretest

This test contains some of the words you will find in this book. It will give you an idea of the kinds of words you will study. When you have completed all the units, the posttest will measure what you have learned.

CHOOSING THE DEFINITIONS

Fill in the bubble next to the item that best defines the word in bold in each sentence.

1. The **aggressive** football player ran through the line and scored.
   - (a.) tired
   - (b.) bold
   - (c.) winning
   - (d.) lucky

2. After the tornado, the neighborhood was covered with **debris**.
   - (a.) sunshine
   - (b.) leaves
   - (c.) reporters
   - (d.) wreckage

3. The workers met with the **administrator** to discuss the new rules.
   - (a.) advertiser
   - (b.) preacher
   - (c.) lawyer
   - (d.) director

4. A brown bear **greedily** rummaged through our groceries.
   - (a.) quickly
   - (b.) selfishly
   - (c.) angrily
   - (d.) shyly

5. The school band gave an **exceptional** performance at the contest.
   - (a.) outstanding
   - (b.) extra
   - (c.) terrible
   - (d.) average

6. Kayla's new ring has a **genuine** diamond.
   - (a.) huge
   - (b.) beautiful
   - (c.) real
   - (d.) artificial

7. The farmer owns one thousand **acres**.
   - (a.) oak trees
   - (b.) units of land
   - (c.) miles
   - (d.) animals

8. The church choir will hold a bake sale in **conjunction** with the spring concert.
   - (a.) association
   - (b.) opposition
   - (c.) advance
   - (d.) evening

9. A deadly **infection** wiped out the state's squirrel population.
   - (a.) weapon
   - (b.) look
   - (c.) disease
   - (d.) hunter

10. In science class, Ryan **disassembled** a telephone.
    - (a.) experimented
    - (b.) took apart
    - (c.) built
    - (d.) dialed

11. His father's advice had an **influence** on John's decision.
    - (a.) power
    - (b.) explanation
    - (c.) thought
    - (d.) memory

12. Conserving energy is good for the earth's **atmosphere**.
    - (a.) oceans
    - (b.) soil
    - (c.) people
    - (d.) air

13. The play was an **absolute** success.
    - (a.) complete
    - (b.) former
    - (c.) unexpected
    - (d.) fake

14. After his high school graduation, Zachary joined the **infantry.**
 (a.) babies   (b.) party   (c.) army   (d.) class

15. Abigail was caught in a storm because she failed to **observe** changes in the sky.
 (a.) ignore   (b.) notice   (c.) wait for   (d.) exit

16. Guards patrolled the **frontier** to keep out illegal visitors.
 (a.) border   (b.) door   (c.) jail   (d.) mountain

17. My **intention** was to finish all my homework before the big game.
 (a.) feeling   (b.) problem   (c.) record   (d.) plan

18. My favorite pet is my colorful male **guppy.**
 (a.) snake   (b.) large parrot   (c.) small fish   (d.) guinea pig

19. Drinking **impure** water can cause serious illness.
 (a.) warm   (b.) dirty   (c.) cold   (d.) bottled

20. During the long, snowy winter, Brianna **yearned** for the sight of a flower.
 (a.) wished   (b.) detested   (c.) searched   (d.) yawned

21. The campers found an **adequate** supply of food at the country grocery store.
 (a.) small   (b.) satisfactory   (c.) tasty   (d.) stale

22. The charity made an **appeal** for donations of canned goods.
 (a.) request   (b.) collection   (c.) feast   (d.) rejection

23. The approach of the huge elephant **alarmed** some of the children.
 (a.) annoyed   (b.) comforted   (c.) growled   (d.) scared

24. The designer found a **novel** solution to the problem.
 (a.) unusual   (b.) common   (c.) practical   (d.) quick

25. We begged Dad to show **mercy** when our pig chewed up his shoe.
 (a.) training   (b.) food   (c.) forgiveness   (d.) thanks

26. The arrival of a skunk caused a **commotion** among the campers.
 (a.) boredom   (b.) disturbance   (c.) peace   (d.) teamwork

27. That baseball player is a spokesperson for the sports drink **industry.**
 (a.) business   (b.) warehouse   (c.) craze   (d.) equipment

28. The program will **conclude** with a speech by the principal.
 (a.) continue   (b.) end   (c.) begin   (d.) feature

29. David **abused** his good clothes by wearing them to play soccer.
 (a.) ironed   (b.) put on   (c.) admired   (d.) mistreated

30. The artist painted quickly, slapping **vivid** spots of color onto the canvas.
  (a.) ugly   (b.) dull   (c.) bright   (d.) round

31. The **incident** at the mall marked the beginning of our friendship.
  (a.) sale   (b.) show   (c.) happening   (d.) contest

32. Exercise improves the **circulation** of blood in our bodies.
  (a.) color   (b.) flow   (c.) cells   (d.) clotting

33. The players on the opposing teams felt **mutual** respect.
  (a.) lack of   (b.) new   (c.) shared   (d.) earned

34. The weather forecaster was **astonished** by the huge snowstorm approaching.
  (a.) amazed   (b.) bored   (c.) buried   (d.) chilled

35. Water began to **seep** through the crack in the pipe.
  (a.) leak   (b.) pour   (c.) cool   (d.) pull

36. Solving the problem calls for the **mentality** of a scientist.
  (a.) books   (b.) computer   (c.) salary   (d.) intellect

37. Olivia's sprained ankle made her an **awkward** dancer.
  (a.) graceful   (b.) ballet   (c.) clumsy   (d.) slow

38. With his father by his side, Anthony felt a sense of **security**.
  (a.) anger   (b.) safety   (c.) fright   (d.) sadness

39. The ancient **legend** explains why giraffes have long necks.
  (a.) tale   (b.) storyteller   (c.) law   (d.) ruin

40. The **course** of the marathon was long and rugged.
  (a.) runner   (b.) route   (c.) time   (d.) race

41. The workers teamed up to **reclaim** the old house.
  (a.) move into   (b.) buy   (c.) fix up   (d.) destroy

42. The hotel staff did everything they could to **accommodate** the guests.
  (a.) scare   (b.) disturb   (c.) feed   (d.) assist

43. Trading in the stock market is one way to **acquire** money.
  (a.) lose   (b.) invest   (c.) get   (d.) donate

44. My aunt and I discussed my **compensation** for the babysitting job.
  (a.) pay   (b.) rules   (c.) time   (d.) children

45. Taking too many risks is **insane** behavior.
  (a.) calm   (b.) pleasant   (c.) usual   (d.) foolish

46. Years ago people read by the light of **kerosene** lamps.
  a. dim **b.** oil **c.** electric **d.** bright

47. The student council made a plan to prevent after-school **combat.**
  a. fights **b.** sports **c.** homework **d.** activities

48. Unfortunately, the plan was **ineffective.**
  a. powerful **b.** outdated **c.** weak **d.** honest

49. Emma's hand felt **numb** after she caught the line drive.
  a. warm **b.** swollen **c.** painful **d.** without feeling

50. It can be hard to **adjust** to a new school when you move.
  a. get used to **b.** be afraid of **c.** be taken to **d.** get out of

51. Reading is an **inexpensive** way to pass the time.
  a. intelligent **b.** useful **c.** economical **d.** exciting

52. Farmers in dry climates need a good **irrigation** system.
  a. cleaning **b.** watering **c.** feeding **d.** cooling

53. James made an **earnest** attempt to apologize.
  a. careless **b.** fake **c.** sad **d.** sincere

54. Justin went over to get **acquainted** with the new neighbor.
  a. forgotten **b.** invited **c.** introduced **d.** ignored

55. "Stop it right now!" Megan growled in a **stern** voice.
  a. soft **b.** harsh **c.** hoarse **d.** friendly

56. The hardware store clerk began to **homogenize** the paint.
  a. mix **b.** pour **c.** stack **d.** remove

57. Alexander set the clothes he would pack on top of the **bureau.**
  a. chest **b.** suitcase **c.** bed **d.** table

58. Grace stayed after school to **oblige** her friend.
  a. call **b.** meet with **c.** ignore **d.** help out

59. The tiny amoeba has only one **cell.**
  a. eye **b.** unit of heat **c.** leg **d.** living unit of matter

60. Would you **classify** a starfish as a plant or an animal?
  a. teach **b.** feed **c.** sort **d.** buy

CHAPTER 1

WORD LIST

Read each word using the pronunciation key.

Group A

abandon (ə ban´ dən)
ambition (am bish´ ən)
century (sen´ chə rē)
debris (də brē´)
guarantee (gâr ən tē´)
ineffective (in ə fek´ tiv)
mentality (men tal´ ə tē)
pneumonia (nŏŏ mōn´ yə)
respectful (ri spekt´ fəl)
temptation (temp tā´ shən)

Group B

annoy (ə noi´)
combat (kom´ bat)
complicate (kom´ plə kāt)
furnish (fər´ nish)
inexpensive (in ik spen´ siv)
mercy (mər´ sē)
pod (pod)
routine (rŏŏ tēn´)
solace (sol´ is)
terrain (tə rān´)

WORD STUDY

Suffixes

The suffixes -er and -or change an action verb into a noun that names a person who performs the action.

actor (ak´ tər) a person who assumes another identity and performs in that role
counselor (koun´ səl ər) a person who is trained to give advice
explorer (ek splor´ ər) a person who travels to investigate a new place
inventor (in vent´ ər) a person who creates something new
manager (man´ ə jər) a person who is in charge of a business or a group of people
writer (rī´ tər) a person who is the author of stories, poems, or articles

Challenge Words

administer (ad min´ əst ər)
camouflage (kam´ ə fläzh)
centennial (sen ten´ ē əl)
combustible (kəm bəs´ t əb əl)
dismal (diz´ məl)

WORDS IN CONTEXT

Read each sentence below to figure out the meaning of the word in **bold**. Use reasoning skills and the remainder of the sentence to help you. Write the meaning of the word on the line.

1. Jacob tried not to let his pesky little sister's teasing **annoy** him.

   _____

2. Emily's **ambition** is to become a famous chess grand master.

   _____

3. Every time I turn on the computer to do my homework, I fight the **temptation** to play a game instead.

   _____

4. Exercise should be a part of everyone's daily **routine**.

   _____

5. On our nature walk, we collected dried flowers, leaves, and **pods**.

   _____

6. If you follow the trail of **debris**, you'll find a giant monster attacking our city.

   _____

7. Some **inexpensive** brands of toothpaste work just as well as the name brands.

   _____

8. A **century** from now, will our grandchildren live in a clean environment?

   _____

9. If you'll **furnish** the cookies, I'll bring the lemonade.

   _____

10. A shouting match is a really **ineffective** way to solve a problem.

    _____

WORD MEANINGS

Word Learning—Group A

Study the spelling, part(s) of speech, and meaning(s) of each word from Group A.
Complete each sentence by writing the word on the line. Then read the sentence.

1. **abandon** *(v.)* 1. to give up control of someone or something; 2. to leave without intending to come back

   Caroline refused to _____ her old friends in the haunted house.

2. **ambition** *(n.)* 1. a desire to achieve a goal; 2. a longing for a position of power

   Robert's _____ drove him to become a star baseball player.

3. **century** *(n.)* a period of 100 years

   What new things will be invented in the next _____?

4. **debris** *(n.)* 1. scattered fragments; 2. ruins; 3. garbage

   After the storm, all the neighbors helped clean up the _____.

5. **guarantee** *(n.)* 1. a promise to fulfill a condition; 2. something that makes certain

   The new computer comes with a one-year _____.

6. **ineffective** *(adj.)* 1. not producing the intended effect; 2. incapable

   Our first plan for setting up a recycling program was _____.

7. **mentality** *(n.)* 1. power of the mind; 2. way of thinking

   Richard needed a detective's _____ to find his lost watch.

8. **pneumonia** *(n.)* a serious lung disease that can cause lung inflammation, high fever, and difficult breathing

   During the winter, many people were hospitalized for _____.

9. **respectful** *(adj.)* showing high regard or esteem

   Brendan speaks to his grandparents in a _____ tone of voice.

10. **temptation** *(n.)* 1. something one wants but perhaps shouldn't have; 2. something one strongly wishes to have

    I have to study, but a day at the beach is a strong _____.

Use Your Vocabulary—Group A

Choose the word from Group A that best completes each sentence. Write the word on the line. You may use the plural form of nouns and the past tense of verbs if necessary.

More than a(n) __1__ ago, before your grandparents were even born, medicine was not as advanced as it is today. Treatment was often __2__, and many patients did not recover. Common diseases such as __3__, or even a bad case of flu, could cause death. Even though doctors couldn't __4__ that their medicine would work, they never __5__ their patients. Doctors working through the night amid the __6__ of earthquakes and other disasters must have felt a strong __7__ to go away and sleep. But most doctors didn't even think of leaving; it is just not part of their __8__. They stayed as long as they were needed. That dedication is one reason that most people are __9__ toward doctors. Many students today whose __10__ is to have a career in medicine were inspired by stories of those long-ago heroes.

1. _____

2. _____

3. _____

4. _____

5. _____

6. _____

7. _____

8. _____

9. _____

10. _____

Word Learning—Group B

Study the spelling, part(s) of speech, and meaning(s) of each word from Group B. Complete each sentence by writing the word on the line. Then read the sentence.

1. **annoy** *(v.)* to irritate or disturb

   The dripping sound of that faucet is beginning to _____ me.

2. **combat** *(n.)* 1. a fight with weapons; 2. any fight or struggle

   The soldiers worked hard so they would be prepared for _____.

3. **complicate** *(v.)* 1. to make difficult; 2. to confuse

   The extra paperwork will only _____ the process.

4. **furnish** *(v.)* 1. to supply or provide; 2. to provide furniture for a room, house, or office

   The money from your taxes will help _____ the new school.

5. **inexpensive** *(adj.)* cheap, low priced

   That _____ coat was made with poor materials.

6. **mercy** *(n.)* 1. showing more kindness than justice requires; 2. lenient, compassionate treatment; 3. something to be thankful for

   The judge showed no _____ when he sentenced the criminal.

7. **pod** *(n.)* a case, shell, or container in which plants form their seeds

   The farmer opened the _____ and found ripe green peas.

8. **routine** *(n.)* a regular course of procedure; *(adj.)* ordinary

   Eating oatmeal is part of our daily morning _____.

   There was nothing _____ about our trip to Antarctica.

9. **solace** *(v.)* to console; *(n.)* relief of sadness

   The coach gave a speech to _____ her team after the loss.

   After arguing with her best friend, Tiffany found _____ in playing a video game with her brother.

10. **terrain** *(n.)* 1. a piece of land; 2. a geographical area

    The campers found it difficult to hike through the rough _____.

Use Your Vocabulary—Group B

Choose the word from Group B that best completes each sentence. Write the word on the line. You may use the plural form of nouns and the past tense of verbs if necessary.

Maybe being a doctor is not your ambition. Have you ever thought about being a park ranger? If you find comfort and **1** in nature, this may be the career for you. Spending time outdoors is part of a ranger's daily **2** . You may find that hikers **3** your job. Many people find hiking through parks a(n) **4** and exciting hobby. It will be your job to **5** aid and information to inexperienced hikers. Hikers may become lost in rugged **6** . They may pick flowers and tramp on rare seed **7** . After all, people and nature are often locked in **8** . But don't let careless hikers **9** you. Have **10** on them. By working with—not against—new hikers, you will teach them to appreciate and protect nature.

1. _____

2. _____

3. _____

4. _____

5. _____

6. _____

7. _____

8. _____

9. _____

10. _____

SYNONYMS

Synonyms are words that have the same or nearly the same meanings.

Part 1 Choose the word from the box that is the best synonym for each group of words. Write the word on the line.

respectful	routine	terrain	ineffective	solace
complicate	mercy	century	mentality	temptation

1. one hundred years, era _____

2. comfort, soothe; consolation, relief _____

3. considerate, polite, admiring _____

4. intellect, mind-set, understanding _____

5. landscape, ground, area _____

6. lure, attraction, bait _____

7. mix up, tangle, make more difficult _____

8. everyday, typical; practice, habit _____

9. pity, extreme kindness, compassion _____

10. worthless, useless _____

Part 2 Replace the underlined word(s) with a word from the box that means the same or almost the same. Write your answer on the line.

guarantee	annoy	pneumonia	abandon	furnish
combat	inexpensive	ambition	debris	pod

11. The company made a <u>promise</u> to have the lowest price. _____

12. The <u>cheap</u> toy broke when I got it home. _____

13. Chad's Chicken Shack will <u>provide</u> uniforms for the team. _____

14. It isn't smart to <u>tease</u> a large lion. _____

15. The leaders signed a treaty to avoid armed <u>conflict</u>. _____

16. Britney had <u>an illness of the lungs</u>. _____

17. The careless campers left <u>trash</u> all over the campsite. _____

18. The twins are as alike as two peas in a <u>shell</u>. _____

19. The climbers had to <u>leave</u> their heavy backpacks. _____

20. Nicolas's <u>goal</u> is to become a teacher. _____

 **ANTONYMS**

Antonyms are words that have opposite or nearly opposite meanings.

Part 1 Choose the word from the box that is the best antonym for each group of words. Write the word on the line.

solace	ambition	furnish
combat	inexpensive	

1. precious, extravagant, costly _____

2. laziness, indifference, lack of purpose _____

3. peace, agreement _____

4. to take away, remove _____

5. grief, sadness _____

Part 2 Replace the underlined word(s) with a word from the box that means the opposite or almost the opposite. Write your answer on the line.

mercy	routine	ineffective
complicate	respectful	

6. Adopting a stray kitten is an act of <u>cruelty</u>. _____

7. The speaker gave <u>rude</u> answers to the students' questions. _____

8. The toddler's help was <u>useful</u>. _____

9. The sound of a siren is <u>extraordinary</u> in the city. _____

10. The extra chores will <u>simplify</u> our life. _____

WORD STUDY

Suffixes Add the suffix *-er* or *-or* to each word. Then write one sentence using the verb form of the word and another sentence using the noun form.

1. write + er _____

_____

_____

2. act + or _____

_____

_____

3. explore + er _____

_____

_____

4. invent + or _____

_____

_____

5. manage + er _____

_____

_____

6. counsel + or _____

_____

_____

CHALLENGE WORDS

Word Learning—Challenge!

Study the spelling, part(s) of speech, and meaning(s) of each word. Complete each sentence by writing the word on the line. Then read the sentence.

1. **administer** *(v.)* 1. to give out; 2. to manage the use of

   The doctors agreed to _____ the flu vaccine for free.

2. **camouflage** *(n.)* a disguise of paint, nets, or foliage that makes something look like its surroundings; *(v.)* to give a false appearance

   The soldiers wore _____ to hide in the woods.

   To _____ her gift, Lucy carried it in a brown paper bag.

3. **centennial** *(adj.)* pertaining to a 100th anniversary; *(n.)* the 100th anniversary

   The mayor planned a _____ celebration for our town.

   The date of the _____ was August 12, 2009.

4. **combustible** *(adj.)* capable of catching fire and burning easily

   Keep all _____ materials away from the bonfire.

5. **dismal** *(adj.)* 1. disastrous, dreadful; 2. gloomy

   We postponed our picnic because of the _____ weather.

Use Your Vocabulary—Challenge!

Party in the Park The park service is throwing a party, and you're in charge. The celebration will honor Dr. Will Curem, the town's first doctor and the person who donated the parkland to the city. It will be held on the 100th anniversary of Dr. Curem's birth. On a separate sheet of paper, write an announcement about the party for your local newspaper. Tell when, where, and why the party will be held. Make the party sound like fun so that many citizens will come. Use the Challenge Words above.

> ### Vocabulary in Action
>
> The word **dismal** can be traced all the way back to medieval calendars. On those calendars, there were two bad or unlucky days marked for every month. The Latin root *mal* appears in many words that are related to "bad" things, such as *malady* ("sickness"), *malice* ("the desire to do bad things to others"), and *malodor* ("bad smell").

13

FUN WITH WORDS

Write the vocabulary word that matches each clue. Put one letter in each blank. Then use the numbered letters to fill in the blanks and solve the riddle.

1. You might cover a lot of this on a hike. ___ ___ ___ ___ ___ ___ ___

        1

2. This makes a promise. ___ ___ ___ ___ ___ ___ ___ ___

          2   3

3. If you're bored, it might be time to change this. ___ ___ ___ ___ ___ ___ ___

        4   5 6

4. If you bring a new chair for the room, you're not furniture. But you do this.

   ___ ___ ___ ___ ___ ___ ___

   7   8

5. What's inside this can keep growing. ___ ___ ___

       9

6. Want to run for president? You'll need lots of this.

   ___ ___ ___ ___ ___ ___ ___

   10   11

7. If something's on sale, it's probably this.

   ___ ___ ___ ___ ___ ___ ___ ___ ___ ___

     12

8. Most people don't see a whole one. ___ ___ ___ ___ ___ ___

      13   14

9. What's left after a big windstorm. ___ ___ ___ ___ ___ ___

     15   16

10. If something doesn't work the way it's supposed to, it's this.

    ___ ___ ___ ___ ___ ___ ___ ___ ___

17 18   19   20   21

Riddle: How can you tell an elephant's been in your refrigerator?

___ ___ ___ ___ ___ ___ ___ ___ ___ ___ ___ ___

19 11 9 1 12 4 17 2 5 16   6 18

___ ___ ___ ___ ___ ___ ___ ___ ___!

20 8 15   10 7 13 3 21 14

CHAPTER 2

WORD LIST

Read each word using the pronunciation key.

Group A

abuse (v. ə byooz´) (n. ə byoos´)
appeal (ə pēl´)
channel (chan´ əl)
compliment (kom´ plə mənt)
distract (dis trakt´)
guppy (gəp´ ē)
infantry (in´ fən trē)
migration (mī grā´ shən)
salvation (sal vā´ shən)
testimony (tes´ tə mō nē)

Group B

accommodate (ə kom´ ə dāt)
charge (chärj)
compassion (kəm pa´ shən)
earnest (ər´ nəst)
infection (in fek´ shən)
inherent (in hir´ ənt)
molecule (mo´ li kyool)
perilous (per´ ə ləs)
sanity (sa´ nə tē)
theory (thē´ ə rē)

WORD STUDY

Homophones

Homophones sound the same, but their spellings and definitions are different.

ascent (ə sent´) a rising or upward movement
assent (ə sent´) an agreement

capital (kap´ ə təl) a large letter; the city that is the seat of government
capitol (kap´ ə təl) the building that houses a state legislature

hangar (haŋ´ ər) a building that houses airplanes
hanger (haŋ´ ər) a piece of shaped metal, wood, or plastic used for holding clothing

Challenge Words
endurance (en dur´ əns)
envious (en´ vē əs)
furrow (fər ō)
mingle (miŋ´ gəl)
modesty (mod´ ə stē)

WORDS IN CONTEXT

Read each sentence below to figure out the meaning of the word in **bold**. Use reasoning skills and the remainder of the sentence to help you. Write the meaning of the word on the line.

1. Do you have an **earnest** desire to work with animals?

   _____

2. A career as a veterinarian can **accommodate** your desire.

   _____

3. If you decide to be a vet, don't let anything **distract** you.

   _____

4. Sometimes being a veterinarian can be **perilous**.

   _____

5. An animal that is usually friendly may **charge** when it is in pain.

   _____

6. Stories of animal **abuse** may upset you.

   _____

7. Some animals will seem to **appeal** to you for help.

   _____

8. But they'll feel fine when you cure their **infection**.

   _____

9. You'll receive **compliments** from happy pet owners.

   _____

10. A dog's wagging tail will be **testimony** that you've chosen the right job.

    _____

WORD MEANINGS

Word Learning—Group A

Study the spelling, part(s) of speech, and meaning(s) of each word. Complete each sentence by writing the word on the line. Then read the sentence.

1. **abuse** *(v.)* 1. to use improperly; 2. to treat cruelly or roughly; *(n.)* 1. cruel or rough treatment; 2. a deceitful act

   If you _____ the privilege, it will be taken away.

   Animal control officers work hard to prevent animal _____.

2. **appeal** *(n.)* an earnest request for help or sympathy; *(v.)* 1. to ask for help; 2. to ask that a case be taken to a higher court in the judicial system

   The director of the food bank made an _____ for donations.

   The lawyer promised to _____ the case to the Supreme Court.

3. **channel** *(n.)* the deeper part of a river or stream; *(v.)* to make a groove

   The ship may run aground if it does not follow the _____.

   Laborers worked for years to _____ a canal to connect the two oceans.

4. **compliment** *(n.)* an admiring remark said about a person or thing

   The teacher's _____ made Hannah blush.

5. **distract** *(v.)* to draw away one's attention to a different object or in many directions at once

   The sound of a TV may _____ you from your reading.

6. **guppy** *(n.)* a tiny fish of tropical fresh water, sometimes kept in aquariums

   If you don't have much room for a pet, try keeping a _____.

7. **infantry** *(n.)* soldiers trained, organized, and equipped to fight on foot

   Dad was awarded a medal for serving in the _____.

8. **migration** *(n.)* moving from one place to another

   Flocks of geese fly in the shape of a wedge during their yearly

   _____.

9. **salvation** *(n.)* 1. a saving; 2. preservation from destruction or failure

   The _____ of swimmers in peril is a lifeguard's most important job.

10. testimony *(n.)* 1. a solemn statement used for evidence or proof; 2. a solemn declaration

Avery was happy to offer _____ that showed his friend could not have committed the crime.

Use Your Vocabulary—Group A

Choose the word from Group A that best completes each sentence. Write the word on the line. You may use the plural form of nouns and the past tense of verbs if necessary.

Michael Gomez always thought he would serve in the _1_ when he grew up. Then he heard a(n) _2_ from a speaker for the National Park Service who was asking for help. "Our parks are in great need of _3_," the speaker said. "If you care about nature and enjoy working outdoors, don't let anything _4_ you from becoming a forest ranger." From that time on, Michael volunteered his time to protect the environment from _5_. At a city council meeting, Michael gave _6_ about saving the city park. He presented a plan to _7_ a canal from the pond to water plants. He made a list of flowers that attract monarch butterflies during their yearly _8_ to Mexico. He offered to organize a sale of goldfish and _9_ to raise money for park improvements. Michael received many _10_ for his conservation work. But the most important thing, Michael knows, is that he is getting experience that will help him in his future career.

1. _____

2. _____

3. _____

4. _____

5. _____

6. _____

7. _____

8. _____

9. _____

10. _____

Vocabulary in Action

"Our inventions are wont to be pretty toys, which **distract** our attention from serious things. They are but improved means to an unimproved end."

—Henry David Thoreau (1817–1862), author, naturalist (from *Walden*)

Word Learning—Group B

Study the spelling, part(s) of speech, and meaning(s) of each word from Group B. Complete each sentence by writing the word on the line. Then read the sentence.

1. **accommodate** *(v.)* 1. to help out; 2. to give something wanted or needed

   The baseball player seemed happy to _____ our desire for an autograph.

2. **charge** *(v.)* 1. to put electricity into; 2. to attack; *(n.)* 1. a price; 2. an accusation

   The computer won't work until you _____ the battery.

   The defendant swore she was not guilty of the _____ of theft.

3. **compassion** *(n.)* pity; sympathy

   The police officer showed _____ for the injured criminal.

4. **earnest** *(adj.)* 1. strong and intense in purpose; 2. eager and serious

   Even though they were playing against the league champions, our team made an _____ effort to win.

5. **infection** *(n.)* disease in humans and animals caused by contact with germs

   Washing your hands often will help you avoid _____.

6. **inherent** *(adj.)* 1. involving a necessary characteristic of something; 2. belonging by nature

   Koalas have an _____ need for eucalyptus leaves.

7. **molecule** *(n.)* the smallest particle of a substance that retains the chemical identity of the substance

   All matter is made up of tiny _____.

8. **perilous** *(adj.)* dangerous

   The rescue effort included a _____ trip across rugged mountains.

9. **sanity** *(n.)* soundness of mind or mental health

   The lawyer hoped to win the case by asking the jurors to question the _____ of the star witness.

10. **theory** *(n.)* 1. an explanation based on observation and reasoning; 2. an opinion or idea

    Every invention begins with a scientific _____.

Use Your Vocabulary—Group B

Choose the word from Group B that best completes each sentence. Write the word on the line. You may use the plural form of nouns and the past tense of verbs if necessary.

When she was a child, Kaitlyn Smith suffered from a serious lung __1__ . Her kindly doctor treated her with humor and __2__ . After she was cured, young Kaitlyn made a(n) __3__ promise to herself to become a doctor. In science class, she studied everything from plants and animals to atoms and __4__ . Medical school seemed so hard and long that she wondered how she would keep from losing her __5__ . But Dr. Smith's desire to help people was __6__ in her character. After many years of studying, she returned to her old neighborhood to set up her practice. Now Dr. Smith does everything she can to __7__ her patients' needs. If her patients cannot pay, she does not __8__ them. She teaches on the latest __9__ about preventing disease. Even though a doctor's job is sometimes __10__ , Kaitlyn Smith would rather be a doctor than anything else.

1. _____

2. _____

3. _____

4. _____

5. _____

6. _____

7. _____

8. _____

9. _____

10. _____

 **SYNONYMS**

Synonyms are words that have the same or nearly the same meanings.

Part 1 Choose the word from the box that is the best synonym for each group of words. Write the word on the line.

distract	accommodate	salvation	abuse	migration
compliment	sanity	molecule	compassion	channel

1. deliverance, rescue, reprieve _____

2. depths; carve _____

3. divert, confuse, lead astray _____

4. good mental health, sense _____

5. hurt, mistreat; injury, misuse _____

6. praise, tribute _____

7. kindness, mercy, respect _____

8. movement, journey, travel _____

9. oblige, assist, help _____

10. unit, particle, bit _____

Part 2 Replace the underlined word(s) with a word from the box that means the same or almost the same. Write your answer on the line.

inherent	appeal	perilous	charge	theory
testimony	infantry	infection	earnest	guppy

11. There will be a small <u>fee</u> for the service. _____

12. Every year charities <u>ask</u> for financial assistance. _____

13. Honesty must be an <u>essential</u> part of a police officer's character.
_____

14. Skydiving is an exciting but <u>risky</u> hobby. _____

15. The doctor said the <u>disease</u> was caused by a virus. _____

16. The scientists devised an experiment to confirm their <u>idea</u>.
_____

17. After graduation, Faith plans to enlist in the <u>army</u>. _____

18. Erica made a <u>solemn</u> promise to do her best work. _____

19. Nathan moved his <u>tropical fish</u> to a new aquarium. _____

20. The witness's <u>statement</u> helped convict the shoplifter. _____

ANTONYMS

Antonyms are words that have opposite or nearly opposite meanings.

Part 1 Choose the word from the box that is the best antonym for each group of words. Write the word on the line.

channel	salvation	distract
earnest	perilous	theory

1. careless, insincere, not serious _____

2. focus, concentrate, emphasize _____

3. safe, easy, secure _____

4. shallows, shore; fill in _____

5. destruction, failure to save _____

6. fact, certainty, truth _____

Part 2 Replace the underlined word(s) with a word from the box that means the opposite or almost the opposite. Write your answer on the line.

accommodate	compliment	sanity	charge
compassion	abuse	migration	

7. Carlos listened to his music teacher's <u>rude comment</u>. _____

8. I know Angelica would never <u>nurture</u> a pig. _____

9. In autumn, many birds begin their yearly <u>staying in one place</u>.

   _____

10. Xavier showed <u>unkindness</u> by talking to the crying man. _____

11. I knew that the growling cougar would <u>retreat</u> if I kept running.

    _____

12. The noise in the lunchroom could make you lose your <u>poor mental health</u>.

    _____

13. The servers do whatever they can to <u>deny</u> guests.

    _____

WORD STUDY

Homophones Proofread the story. Circle each word that is used incorrectly. Then rewrite the incorrect sentences on the lines below using the correct words.

Our class begged the principal to allow us to take a class trip. The principal gave her ascent—but only if we raised the money ourselves. We held many fundraisers. Our best one was a craft sale. We sold useful things such as hangars covered with ribbons. We washed cars. We even washed small airplanes in their hangers at the local airport. At last we had enough money to fly to our nation's capitol. As our plane made its assent, we all cheered. We couldn't wait to visit the White House and the Capital Building.

1. _____

2. _____

3. _____

4. _____

5. _____

6. _____

CHALLENGE WORDS

Word Learning—Challenge!

Study the spelling, part(s) of speech, and meaning(s) of each word. Complete each sentence by writing the word on the line. Then read the sentence.

1. **endurance** *(n.)* the ability to withstand hardship

    Marathon runners need both strength and _____.

2. **envious** *(adj.)* feeling dissatisfaction because of wanting what another has

    Alejandra tried not to be _____ of her sister's musical talent.

3. **furrow** *(n.)* long, narrow groove, as cut in the earth by a plow; *(v.)* to wrinkle

    The farmer began preparing the field by making a _____.

    Every time the twins concentrate, they both _____ their brows in the same way.

4. mingle *(v.)* 1. to bring or mix together; 2. to associate

Serena breathed a sigh of relief as her party guests began to relax and

_____.

5. modesty *(n.)* 1. not thinking highly of oneself or one's abilities; 2. being shy

Gregory's _____ kept him from bragging about winning the
science fair.

Use Your Vocabulary—Challenge!

I Have a Dream Michael Gomez and Kaitlyn Smith each had a dream. They planned
ahead to achieve their goals. What career sounds interesting to you? What will it take
to fulfill your dream? On a separate sheet of paper, write about things you can do now
that will help you achieve your goal. Use the Challenge Words below.

endurance	envious	furrow	mingle	modesty

FUN WITH WORDS

Use a vocabulary word to complete each sentence. The word you choose should rhyme
with the word in *italics*.

1. Perhaps you'll accuse me of *vanity*, but I never question my _____.

2. I'd rather have a *puppy*, but I'll settle for a(n) _____.

3. I don't have powers of *detection*, but this fever says I have a(n) _____.

4. My bank account isn't *large*, so I can't afford that _____.

5. This summer's *vacation* will be my _____.

Now you try it. On a separate sheet of paper, write rhyming sentences using three of
the following vocabulary words.

appeal	theory	distract	channel	abuse

CHAPTER 3

WORD LIST

Read each word using the pronunciation key.

Group A

abolish (ə bol´ ish)
accumulate (ə kyōō´ myə lāt)
circulation (sər kyə lā´ shən)
conclude (kən klōōd´)
harmonize (här´ mə nīz)
inflammable (in flam´ ə bəl)
nourish (nər´ ish)
prediction (pri dik´ shən)
satellite (sat´ ə līt)
traitor (trā´ tər)

Group B

adequate (ad´ i kwət)
astonish (ə ston´ ish)
circumference (sər kum´ frəns)
conjunction (kən junk´ shən)
hoarse (hôrs)
influence (in´ flōō əns)
novel (nov´ əl)
preserve (pri zərv´)
scandal (skan´ dəl)
treaty (trē´ tē)

WORD STUDY

Prefixes

The prefix *tele-* means "far away."

telecommunicate (tel´ ə kə myōō nə kāt) to send electronic messages over distances
telephone (tel´ ə fōn) a machine for sending and receiving speech sounds over distances
telephoto (tel´ ə fō tō) a camera lens that makes distant objects appear to be closer
telescope (tel´ ə skōp) an instrument that makes distant objects appear to be closer
television (tel´ ə vizh ən) a receiver for sound and pictures that are sent over the airwaves

Challenge Words

antiquated (ant´ ə kwāt əd)
compile (kəm pīl´)
deficient (di fish´ ənt)
dependent (di pen´ dənt)
saturate (sach´ ə rāt)

WORDS IN CONTEXT

Read each sentence below to figure out the meaning of the word in **bold**. Use reasoning skills and the remainder of the sentence to help you. Write the meaning of the word on the line.

1. Every subject in school helps you **accumulate** knowledge.

   _____

2. Our teacher assigns us biographies to read, but I would much rather read **novels**.

   _____

3. If **satellites** fascinate you, you will probably find astronomy most interesting.

   _____

4. In science, you may study the body's blood **circulation** system.

   _____

5. Even if you're not a great cook, you can learn to make an **adequate** meal in the new cooking class.

   _____

6. You may learn things in your social studies class that will **astonish** you.

   _____

7. History is filled with exciting adventures and mysterious **scandals**.

   _____

8. One of the most famous historical facts involved the duel of the well-known **traitor** Benedict Arnold.

   _____

9. Have you learned to measure the **circumference** of a circle in math class yet?

   _____

10. Students may joke that someone should **abolish** school, but without school, where would you learn so many interesting things?

   _____

WORD MEANINGS

Word Learning—Group A

Study the spelling, part(s) of speech, and meaning(s) of each word from Group A. Complete each sentence by writing the word on the line. Then read the sentence.

1. **abolish** *(v.)* to do away with or put an end to

   I hope our school board does not _____ the drama program.

2. **accumulate** *(v.)* to pile up or collect

   It takes a long time and hard work to _____ a fortune.

3. **circulation** *(n.)* going around or sending around

   Veins and arteries are part of our body's _____ system.

4. **conclude** *(v.)* 1. to end; 2. to make decisions or opinions by reasoning

   The meeting will _____ after the president's speech.

5. **harmonize** *(v.)* 1. to add tones to a melody to create chords; 2. to play or sing to a tuneful sound

   The barbershop quartet gets together to _____ weekly.

6. **inflammable** *(adj.)* 1. easily set on fire; 2. easily excited or angered

   Never light a match near an _____ fluid, such as gasoline.

7. **nourish** *(v.)* 1. to help grow, or keep alive and well, with food; 2. to maintain

   This plant food is just what we need to _____ the seedlings.

8. **prediction** *(n.)* something told beforehand

   The coach made a _____ that our team would win.

9. **satellite** *(n.)* 1. a celestial body that revolves around a planet; 2. a moon; 3. a manufactured object intended to circle a planet

   Soon NASA will launch a new communications _____.

10. **traitor** *(n.)* 1. a person who betrays a trust, a duty, or a friend; 2. one who commits treason

   The counterspy admitted that he was a _____ to his country.

Use Your Vocabulary—Group A

Choose the word from Group A that best completes each sentence. Write the word on the line. You may use the plural form of nouns and the past tense of verbs if necessary.

The moon is a(n) __1__ of our planet. For centuries, people made __2__ about what we would find on the moon. Some people __3__ that it was made of green cheese. Finally, the Apollo astronauts were sent to find out what was there. With a fiery burst of __4__ fuel, the rocket was launched. The crew's mission was to __5__ myths about the moon. They __6__ samples of soil and moon rocks. They planned to find out if the moon could support and __7__ any form of life. The astronauts had fun too. Some mornings the ground crew would __8__ in a cheerful wake-up tune. Because the moon has less gravity, the astronauts could jump and play. The lack of air in __9__ on the moon means the footprints they made will never blow away. Only a(n) __10__ would refuse to be proud of our brave astronauts.

1. _____

2. _____

3. _____

4. _____

5. _____

6. _____

7. _____

8. _____

9. _____

10. _____

Word Learning—Group B

Study the spelling, part(s) of speech, and meaning(s) of each word from Group B. Complete each sentence by writing the word on the line. Then read the sentence.

1. **adequate** *(adj.)* enough; sufficient

   Did we pack an _____ supply of food for the trip?

2. **astonish** *(v.)* to surprise greatly, amaze

   The magician's trick will _____ the audience.

3. **circumference** *(n.)* the distance around a circle or sphere

   The earth's _____ is about 25,000 miles.

4. **conjunction** *(n.)* 1. a joining of something with another; 2. union; 3. combination

   The final plan was a _____ of both ideas.

5. **hoarse** *(adj.)* 1. rough and deep sounding; 2. having a harsh voice

   After the big game, our voices were _____ from cheering.

6. influence *(n.)* the act or power of producing an effect without great force

Mom hopes the babysitter will be a good _____ on us.

7. novel *(adj.)* of a new kind; *(n.)* often long, usually complex fictional story

Madison thought of a _____ solution for the problem.

Would you rather read a _____ or a history?

8. preserve *(v.)* 1. to keep safe from harm or change; 2. to protect or maintain

Mom planned to _____ my picture by framing it.

9. scandal *(n.)* 1. conduct that brings disgrace or shocks the public; 2. the loss of or damage to reputation

The newspaper reported the shocking _____.

10. treaty *(n.)* 1. a written, formal agreement between countries; 2. the document that contains the agreement

The heads of state held a meeting to sign the peace _____.

Use Your Vocabulary—Group B

Choose the word from Group B that best completes each sentence. Write the word on the line. You may use the plural form of nouns and the past tense of verbs if necessary.

It seems that there is __1__ room in outer space for everyone. After all, many natural and human-made objects travel around the earth's __2__ without getting in one another's way. But maybe now is the time to draw up a(n) __3__ among the nations to make rules to __4__ outer space as we know it. Already people have had some __5__ ideas for using outer space. Advertisers have suggested working in __6__ with the government to launch a giant lighted billboard into the sky. Are you shocked? Does that idea __7__ you? They think this advertising would have a great __8__ on consumers. Most people I know would shout themselves __9__ fighting that plan. Imagine gazing up at the stars on a warm summer night and seeing a commercial instead! I think advertising in space would be a(n) __10__. Don't you?

1. _____

2. _____

3. _____

4. _____

5. _____

6. _____

7. _____

8. _____

9. _____

10. _____

SYNONYMS

Synonyms are words that have the same or nearly the same meanings.

Part 1 Choose the word from the box that is the best synonym for each group of words. Write the word on the line.

inflammable	harmonize	accumulate	influence	satellite
conjunction	circumference	circulation	nourish	conclude

1. association, joining _____

2. authority, control, power _____

3. end, finish; decide _____

4. distribution, rotation, flow _____

5. combustible, explosive, excitable _____

6. moon, space station _____

7. perimeter, distance around _____

8. gather, store, amass _____

9. sustain, feed, support _____

10. be tuneful or melodious _____

Part 2 Replace the underlined word(s) with a word from the box that means the same or almost the same. Write your answer on the line.

scandal	preserve	novel	hoarse	treaty
abolish	traitor	adequate	astonish	prediction

11. The secret I am about to tell you will <u>amaze</u> you. _____

12. The <u>pact</u> was signed, and the countries declared peace. _____

13. The student who stole our unicorn mascot is a <u>betrayer</u>! _____

14. The mayor's bad behavior is a <u>disgrace</u> to our town. _____

15. People of all races worked to <u>put an end to</u> slavery. _____

16. Cameron thinks his grades are <u>satisfactory</u>. _____

17. The weather reporter's <u>forecast</u> turned out to be wrong. _____

18. Nicole woke up with a cold and a <u>ragged</u> voice. _____

19. The citizens planned a drive to <u>keep</u> the historic building. _____

20. Writing a <u>long, fictional story</u> is a hard job. _____

ANTONYMS

Antonyms are words that have opposite or nearly opposite meanings.

Part 1 Choose the word from the box that is the best antonym for each group of words. Write the word on the line.

accumulate	scandal	hoarse
conjunction	novel	traitor

1. distribute, scatter, give away _____

2. patriot, loyalist, nationalist _____

3. typical, usual, familiar _____

4. splitting apart, separation _____

5. smooth sounding, soft _____

6. good behavior, propriety _____

> ## Vocabulary in Action
>
> The word *invisible* means "not visible." The word *ineffective* means "not effective." They both use the prefix *in-* to mean "not." But just as words can have more than one meaning, some prefixes have more than one meaning. The prefix *in-* can also mean "inside." For example, *inscribe* means "to write inside something," and *inherent* describes a quality inside something. The word **inflammable** uses the prefix *in-* to mean "inside." Sometimes people think *inflammable* means "not able to be set on fire." In fact, *inflammable* and *flammable* mean the same thing!

Part 2 Replace the underlined word with a word from the box that means the opposite or almost the opposite. Write your answer on the line.

adequate	conclude	inflammable
nourish	abolish	astonish

7. Mom sprinkled a <u>fireproof</u> liquid over the stove. _____

8. Dad prepared a meal that could <u>starve</u> an army. _____

9. The end of the movie will <u>bore</u> you. _____

10. The candidate vowed to <u>create</u> high taxes. _____

11. The game will <u>begin</u> when the final buzzer sounds. _____

12. The detectives found <u>insufficient</u> information to name a suspect.

_____

 WORD STUDY

Prefixes Write a sentence for each item. Use one word from the box in each sentence.

telephone	telecommunicate	telephoto
telescope	television	

1. You are watching your favorite weekly show. You are sitting on the couch in your living room. Write a sentence to tell what you are doing.

_____

2. You've heard that a comet is passing over your city. You go out on the back porch, but then you realize that you can't see the comet with your naked eye. Write a sentence to tell what you can use to see the comet.

_____

3. You hear a ringing sound. Then you talk to your grandmother who lives in another town. Write a sentence to tell what you are using to talk to your grandmother.

_____

4. Your friend has finally stood up on water skis! You want to take a picture to prove it, but you are onshore and your friend is in the middle of the lake. Write a sentence to tell how you will take the picture.

_____

5. You think of something you want to tell your friend. But you're not allowed to talk on the phone this late. You can send an e-mail, though. Write a sentence to tell what you will do.

_____

CHALLENGE WORDS

Word Learning—Challenge!

Study the spelling, part(s) of speech, and meaning(s) of each word. Complete each sentence by writing the word on the line. Then read the sentence.

1. antiquated *(adj.)* 1. out of date; 2. out of style

The company's productivity was low because of _____ manufacturing methods.

2. compile *(v.)* 1. to collect and bring together; 2. to build up gradually

Throughout the year, the teacher will _____ a book of the students' best writing samples.

3. deficient *(adj.)* lacking a needed element or quality

A diet of ice cream would be _____ in vitamins.

4. dependent *(adj.)* trusting or relying on another; *(n.)* one who relies on another for support

The date of the picnic is _____ on the weather.

As long as you live at home, you will be a _____ of your parents.

5. saturate *(v.)* 1. to fill completely; 2. to soak

The heavy downpour will soon _____ the ground.

Use Your Vocabulary—Challenge!

Here's What I Think! The article that uses the Group B words on page 29 is an editorial. The writer wrote the article to express an opinion. On a separate sheet of paper, write your own editorial about an issue you feel strongly about. Use the Challenge Words below.

antiquated	compile	deficient	dependent	saturate

 FUN WITH WORDS

Find and circle each word hidden in the puzzle below. Words may be horizontal, vertical, or diagonal. Some are spelled backwards.

abolish	adequate	astonish	conclude	hoarse
nourish	novel	prediction	scandal	traitor

```
L J U H T V O U S C A M S L A
A A D E Q U A T E I B N O V S
D B H P R E C M B R O H A R J
E O S O S A S T O N I S H F N
Q L I B A R N E K O W Q U T Y
L I R N U G K R O P J K D E E
S S U A R G U I G O L T H D D
B H O A R S E V X S D E L Q U
T M N B G R T Y U J M L V L L
P R E D I T Y E G I O N L O C
A H E A D P R E D I C T I O N
J O I A M A L A D N A C S F O
A E I H T L O T H U V W R T C
I N F L U Y G T R A I T O R S
```

Review 1–3

Word Meanings Fill in the bubble of the word that is best defined by each phrase.

1. an object that circles a planet
   - (a.) treaty
   - (b.) scandal
   - (c.) satellite
   - (d.) molecule

2. relating to an essential characteristic of something
   - a. earnest
   - (b.) inherent
   - (c.) hoarse
   - (d.) perilous

3. one who betrays another
   - (a.) theory
   - (b.) solace
   - (c.) terrain
   - (d.) traitor

4. protection from destruction
   - (a.) compassion
   - (b.) salvation
   - (c.) circulation
   - (d.) charge

5. a seed vessel
   - (a.) pod
   - (b.) guppy
   - (c.) infection
   - (d.) conjunction

6. a serious statement
   - (a.) testimony
   - (b.) prediction
   - (c.) abuse
   - (d.) combat

7. a formal agreement between countries
   - (a.) terrain
   - (b.) mercy
   - (c.) circumference
   - (d.) treaty

8. to request help
   - (a.) appeal
   - (b.) accommodate
   - (c.) nourish
   - (d.) complicate

9. a reasonable explanation
   - (a.) charge
   - (b.) century
   - (c.) influence
   - (d.) theory

10. shocking behavior
    - (a.) migration
    - (b.) scandal
    - (c.) infantry
    - (d.) conjunction

11. overwhelming kindness and justice
    - (a.) channel
    - (b.) novel
    - (c.) mercy
    - (d.) pneumonia

12. easy to burn
    - (a.) inflammable
    - (b.) respectful
    - (c.) hoarse
    - (d.) influence

13. good enough
    - (a.) routine
    - (b.) earnest
    - (c.) novel
    - (d.) adequate

14. to treat badly or unkindly
    - (a.) abolish
    - (b.) abuse
    - (c.) harmonize
    - (d.) astonish

15. bits and pieces left after destruction
    - (a.) debris
    - (b.) mercy
    - (c.) prediction
    - (d.) terrain

Sentence Completion

Choose the word from Part 1 that best completes each of the following sentences. Write the word in the blank. Then do the same for Part 2. You will not use all the words.

Part 1

routine	sanity	guarantee	inexpensive
ineffective	mentality	preserve	temptation

1. I always have to fight the _____ to ride my bicycle when I should be doing homework.

2. My bike is nothing fancy—just a(n) _____ model—but I love to ride it in my neighborhood.

3. For me, a bicycle ride is never _____; it's always an adventure.

4. My mom says I like my bike so much that I have a "bicycling _____."

5. I hope to _____ my love of bikes throughout my life.

Part 2

annoy	furnished	earnest	accumulate
perilous	respectful	concluded	ambition

6. My _____ desire is to become a professional bicycle racer.

7. It can be _____ work—some of the courses are risky and difficult.

8. When my mom heard that, she _____ that she didn't want her daughter racing bikes.

9. Becoming a professional racer is my true _____, so finally Mom said I can enter some of the beginners' races.

10. Eventually, I will _____ enough experience to move up to more advanced races.

Synonyms

Synonyms Synonyms are words that have the same or nearly the same meanings. Choose the word from the box that is the best synonym for each group of words. Write your answer on the line.

charge	migration	infection	ineffective	circulation
conjunction	influence	abandon	complicate	

1. movement, journey, travel _____

2. leave, give up, forsake _____

3. association, joining _____

4. disease, illness, plague _____

5. distribution, rotation, flow _____

6. confuse, tangle, make more difficult _____

7. amount, fee; accuse, attack _____

8. authority, control, power _____

9. worthless, useless, weak _____

Antonyms

Antonyms Antonyms are words that have opposite or nearly opposite meanings. Choose the word from the box that is the best antonym for each group of words. Write your answer on the line.

nourish	sanity	distract	compliment	combat
abolish	novel	annoy	solace	

1. focus, concentrate, emphasize _____

2. typical, usual, familiar _____

3. blame, disturb; grief, sadness _____

4. poor mental health _____

5. leave in peace, not bother   _____

6. insult, rude comment   _____

7. peace, agreement   _____

8. starve, deprive, neglect   _____

9. create, make, establish   _____

Word Riddles Choose the word from the box that answers the riddle. Write it on the line.

astonish	guppy	respectful	century
molecule	prediction	harmonize	pneumonia

1. I am a verb.
I mean "to surprise or amaze."
I am an antonym of *bore.*

I am _____.

2. I am a noun.
You might find me at a hospital.
I begin with a silent letter.

I am _____.

3. I am a noun.
You might find me in a science lab.
I am a tiny bit or particle.

I am _____.

4. I am a verb.
I am what people do when they sing together.
I end with a suffix.

I am _____.

5. I am a noun.
I rhyme with *affliction.*
I am a synonym of *forecast* or *prognosis.*

I am _____.

6. I am a noun.
You might find me in your aquarium.
I rhyme with *puppy,* but I don't walk on a leash.

I am _____.

7. I am an adjective.
I describe your feeling for someone you admire.
I end with a suffix.

I am _____.

8. I am a noun.
I'm often spoken of at a celebration.
I mean "a period of 100 years."

I am _____.

WORD LIST

Read each word using the pronunciation key.

Group A

acquaint (ə kwānt´)
atmosphere (at´ məs fēr)
clarify (klâr´ ə fī)
conscience (kon´ shəns)
encounter (in koun´ tər)
homogenize (hə moj´ ə nīz)
nimble (nim´ bəl)
progress (*n.* prog´ res) (*v.* prə gres´)
scheme (skēm)
triumphant (trī um´ fənt)

Group B

acquire (ə kwīr´)
annual (an´ yo͞o wəl)
classic (klas´ ik)
consist (kən sist´)
exceptional (ik sep´ shən əl)
injection (in jek´ shən)
nuisance (no͞o´ səns)
prompt (prompt)
security (si kyo͞or´ ə tē)
uncivilized (un siv´ ə līzd)

WORD STUDY

Irregular Plurals

Plural words that do not end in *s* or *es* are called irregular plurals.

bacteria (bak tēr´ ē ə) microscopic living things *Singular:* **bacterium**
brothers-in-law (bruth´ ərz-in-lô) the brothers of a spouse or the husbands of sisters *Singular:* **brother-in-law**
crises (krī´ sēz) turning points *Singular:* **crisis**
oxen (oks´ ən) animals that are a kind of cattle *Singular:* **ox**
teeth (tēth) white, bonelike growths found in the mouth and used for chewing; projections *Singular:* **tooth**
women (wi´ mən) adult females of the human species *Singular:* **woman**

Challenge Words

devout (di vout´)
dwindle (dwin´ dəl)
exempt (ig zempt´)
impenetrable (im pen´ i trə bəl)
recur (ri kər´)

WORDS IN CONTEXT

Read each sentence below to figure out the meaning of the word in **bold**. Use reasoning skills and the remainder of the sentence to help you. Write the meaning of the word on the line.

1. Joshua gave a **triumphant** dance after scoring the touchdown.

   _____

2. My little sister follows us around and makes a general **nuisance** of herself.

   _____

3. The doctor held up the needle and said, "This **injection** won't hurt a bit."

   _____

4. You have to be **nimble** to do skate tricks.

   _____

5. Kevin is always coming up with some clever **scheme** to help people.

   _____

6. Amanda's starring role showed that she was an **exceptional** actor for someone so young.

   _____

7. Pat is always **prompt** when he goes to a movie because he hates to miss the beginning.

   _____

8. A tour of the White House will **acquaint** you with important objects from our country's history.

   _____

9. Water **consists** of a combination of oxygen and hydrogen.

   _____

10. It's always fun to go to art class because the **atmosphere** is informal and friendly.

   _____

WORD MEANINGS

Word Learning—Group A

Study the spelling, part(s) of speech, and meaning(s) of each word from Group A.
Complete each sentence by writing the word on the line. Then read the sentence.

1. **acquaint** *(v.)* 1. to make known; 2. to inform; 3. to familiarize

   Take some time to _____ yourself with the new computers
   before you begin working.

2. **atmosphere** *(n.)* 1. the mass of air that surrounds the earth; 2. a surrounding
   influence

   Earth is the only known planet with an _____ that supports
   life.

3. **clarify** *(v.)* 1. to make clear or easy to understand; 2. to explain

   This diagram will help _____ the process for you.

4. **conscience** *(n.)* the sense within you that tells you when you are doing right
   or wrong

   Jeffrey had a guilty _____ until he confessed his lie.

5. **encounter** *(v.)* 1. to meet by chance; 2. to be faced with; *(n.)* 1. an unexpected
   meeting; 2. a meeting of enemies

   Bailey was surprised to _____ an acquaintance from home on
   her vacation in a distant state.

   Francisco's sudden _____ with the large, friendly ape left him
   surprised but unhurt.

6. **homogenize** *(v.)* to blend different elements so they are evenly mixed

   To make milk more healthy to drink, the dairies _____ it
   before shipping it to the store.

7. **nimble** *(adj.)* 1. moving with agility; 2. active and sure-footed; 3. quick

   The _____ goat easily hopped across the high, rocky hill
   without slipping or falling.

8. **progress** *(n.)* 1. movement toward a goal; 2. an advance; growth; *(v.)* 1. to move
   forward; 2. to proceed

   Kylie is making steady _____ in her study of Japanese.

   After a short delay for refueling, we were able to _____ on our
   journey across the continent.

9. scheme *(n.)* 1. a plan of action; 2. a plot

If a money-making _____ sounds too good to be true, it probably is.

10. triumphant *(adj.)* 1. victorious; 2. winning; 3. rejoicing for success at a victory

We cheered as the players on the _____ team left the field.

Use Your Vocabulary—Group A

Choose the word from Group A that best completes each sentence. Write the word on the line. You may use the plural form of nouns and the past tense of verbs if necessary.

Last night I dreamed I had a(n) __1__ with space creatures. I asked them about their background to better __2__ myself with these creatures. One creature explained that their __3__ was to land on the moon, but their spaceship had gotten off course. Sometimes I couldn't understand the creature's speech, so he drew a picture to __4__ what he said. Their mission was to learn how to __5__ their own dairy products—they'd heard that the moon was made of green cheese. After informing the aliens that grocery stores carry cheese, one creature made a __6__ leap high into the branches of a tree. He was surprised to learn that the gravity in the earth's __7__ made jumping so easy. We decided to go to the grocery store, but the weight of the spaceship in my truck made our __8__ slow. "Our mission is __9__!" the creatures yelled in unison. They left that night, but my __10__ still bothers me. I didn't tell them that the moon is not really made of cheese.

1. _____

2. _____

3. _____

4. _____

5. _____

6. _____

7. _____

8. _____

9. _____

10. _____

Vocabulary in Action

The word **homogenize** can be used to talk about mixing many things. The best-known use of homogenization is in milk processing. Fresh, unprocessed milk separates on its own. The cream floats to the top, and water stays at the bottom. To keep milk from separating into water and cream, most dairies homogenize it. This explains why your first glass of rich, white milk will taste the same the next day too.

Word Learning—Group B

Study the spelling, part(s) of speech, and meaning(s) of each word from Group B. Complete each sentence by writing the word on the line. Then read the sentence.

1. acquire *(v.)* 1. to gain possession of something; 2. to get

The museum director hoped to _____ a famous painting at the auction.

2. annual *(adj.)* done or performed once a year; *(n.)* a plant that survives for one year or one season

Chelsea can't wait for our _____ math competition.

That _____ is so pretty that we will plant another one next spring.

3. classic *(adj.)* 1. of high value or quality; 2. excellent; 3. traditional; *(n.)* a work of great excellence

The model with the huge fins is a _____ example of car design in the 1950s.

That thrilling novel is a real _____.

4. consist *(v.)* to be made up of

Doubleheaders _____ of two separate baseball games.

5. exceptional *(adj.)* 1. unusual; 2. varying from the norm

The teacher's note says that Mya is an _____ math student.

6. injection *(n.)* the act or process of forcing liquid through a hollow needle

The doctor gave Ashley an _____ of the vaccine.

7. nuisance *(n.)* a thing or person that is annoying or disagreeable

A tiny mosquito can be a big _____.

8. prompt *(adj.)* on time; *(v.)* to move to action without delay

Savanna sent a _____ reply to my invitation.

An alarm clock may _____ Martin to get out of bed each day.

9. security *(n.)* 1. freedom from danger; 2. a feeling of being safe

The return of their mother gave the lion cubs a sense of _____.

10. uncivilized *(adj.)* 1. savage; 2. remote from settled areas

Be sure to pack plenty of supplies if travelling in _____ territory.

Use Your Vocabulary—Group B

Choose the word from Group B that best completes each sentence. Write the word on the line. You may use the plural form of nouns and the past tense of verbs if necessary.

My father has a(n) __1__ 1925 Packard without a scratch on it. He __2__ the car five years ago from his friend. Dad keeps that car in __3__ condition. He parks it in a locked garage with a good __4__ system. Once a year, though, he takes the family to the __5__ antique car show in Detroit. You might think a car show would be a big mess, but think again. There is nothing __6__ about it. Everything is precisely planned. The show __7__ of three parts: the parade of cars, the judging and awarding of prizes, and an auction. One year we were late because we had to take our iguana to the vet for a(n)__8__. Since then, we've always been careful to be __9__. Towing the old Packard to Detroit can be a(n) __10__, but the show is so much fun that it's worth it!

1. _____

2. _____

3. _____

4. _____

5. _____

6. _____

7. _____

8. _____

9. _____

10. _____

SYNONYMS

Synonyms are words that have the same or nearly the same meanings.

Part 1 Choose the word from the box that is the best synonym for each group of words. Write the word on the line.

classic	homogenize	atmosphere	acquaint	scheme
clarify	consist	injection	uncivilized	encounter

1. not settled, crude, wild _____

2. air; sense, surroundings _____

3. define, explain, interpret _____

4. high quality, traditional; masterpiece _____

5. strategy, purpose, method _____

6. contain, include, involve _____

7. unexpected meeting; meeting of enemies _____

8. shot, dose, treatment _____

9. introduce, tell, advise _____

10. mix, blend _____

Part 2 Replace the underlined word(s) with a word from the box that means the same or almost the same. Write your answer on the line.

acquire	annual	exceptional	prompt	nuisance
progress	nimble	security	triumphant	conscience

11. Pedro hopes to <u>earn</u> enough money to get a new bike. _____

12. The school installed a new <u>protection</u> system. _____

13. We are planning our <u>yearly</u> vacation now. _____

14. This graph shows the <u>growth</u> of the business last year. _____

15. My <u>inner voice</u> warned me not to leave the job undone. _____

16. Miriam expected a <u>timely</u> answer to her question. _____

17. Guadalupe has an <u>outstanding</u> talent for drawing. _____

18. Moses felt <u>successful</u> the first time he rode his rollerblades all the way down the hill without falling. _____

19. Chores can be a <u>bother</u>, but they have to be done. _____

20. The <u>graceful</u> dancer leaped high into the air. _____

Vocabulary in Action

Atmosphere comes from the Latin words *atmos* (vapor) and *spharia* (sphere). When the word first appeared in English, people talked about it in reference to the air surrounding the moon. Later, scientists realized that the moon does not have an atmosphere. Today, many scientists believe the moon is surrounded by thin molecules. These molecules are similar to—but not exactly the same as—an atmosphere.

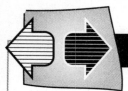

ANTONYMS

Antonyms are words that have opposite or nearly opposite meanings.

Part 1 Choose the word from the box that is the best antonym for each group of words. Write the word on the line.

nuisance	nimble	triumphant
exceptional	security	prompt

1. beaten, defeated _____

2. feeling of danger, risk, hazard _____

3. delight, pleasure, comfort _____

4. tardy, late _____

5. clumsy, awkward, slow _____

6. common, ordinary, usual _____

Part 2 Replace the underlined word(s) with a word from the box that means the opposite or almost the opposite. Write your answer on the line.

progress	uncivilized	acquire
clarify	classic	encounter

7. The scientists planned to explore <u>settled</u> territory. _____

8. Did my explanation <u>muddle</u> the situation? _____

9. Wendy hopes to <u>avoid</u> her friend at the mall. _____

10. Nickolas thinks my new song is <u>forgettable</u>. _____

11. Mom has said that we will <u>give up</u> more chores as we get older.

   _____

12. My little sister hopes to <u>fall back</u> to a two-wheeler this spring.

   _____

> ## Notable Quotes
>
> "Behold the turtle. He makes **progress** only when he sticks his neck out."
>
> —James Bryant Conant (1893–1978), chemist, educator, politician

WORD STUDY

Irregular Plurals Read each sentence. Then write a sentence that uses the plural form of the word in **bold**.

1. When I saw her from a distance, I didn't realize that the **woman** was my mother.

   _____

2. Bryant claims that he is as strong as an **ox**.

   _____

3. We looked at a one-celled **bacterium** under the microscope.

   _____

4. When Keaton marries my sister Clara, I will have a new **brother-in-law**.

   _____

5. The dentist was able to save the **tooth** Ashton almost lost in the bicycle accident.

   _____

6. The first day of school may feel like a **crisis** to a kindergartner's parents.

   _____

CHALLENGE WORDS

Word Learning—Challenge!

Study the spelling, part(s) of speech, and meaning(s) of each word. Complete each sentence by writing the word on the line. Then read the sentence.

1. **devout** *(adj.)* 1. earnest; 2. serious; 3. devoted to religion

   The _____ church members attended the meeting.

2. **dwindle** *(v.)* 1. to become less; 2. to shrink

   As our food supply began to _____, we anxiously waited for the snowplow's arrival.

3. **exempt** *(v.)* to release from a duty or rule; *(adj.)* free or released from a duty or rule

   The teacher promised to _____ band members from the homework assignment on the night of the concert.

   In some states, food items are _____ from a sales tax.

4. **impenetrable** *(adj.)* incapable of being pierced, entered, or passed

   Lesly warned us to avoid wandering into the _____ forest.

5. **recur** *(v.)* 1. to be repeated; 2. to come up again for consideration

   The disease may _____ if you don't get enough rest.

Use Your Vocabulary—Challenge!

An Exceptional Experience Think about an experience you've had or would like to have. Then write about your experience on a separate sheet of paper. You might write about a real experience, such as a trip to a car show, or a fantastic experience, such as an encounter with space aliens. Use the Challenge Words below.

exempt	recur	impenetrable	dwindle	devout

FUN WITH WORDS

Stranded! You were out for a peaceful boat ride when a sudden storm forced you to abandon ship. Fortunately, you were able to struggle to shore on a deserted island. You have one bottle in which you can put a message telling what has happened and asking for help. Make your message clear and brief, but use at least eight of the words below.

acquire	progress	uncivilized	encounter
consist	triumphant	nuisance	nimble
scheme	security	prompt	acquaint

_____

_____

_____

_____

CHAPTER 5

WORD LIST

Read each word using the pronunciation key.

Group A

acre (ā′ kər)
classify (klas′ ə fī)
contemplate (kon′ təm plāt)
explore (ik splôr′)
ideal (ī dēl′)
insane (in sān′)
numb (num)
protein (prō′ tēn)
sentimental (sen tə men′ təl)
unexpected (un ik spek′ tid)

Group B

awkward (ôk′ wərd)
clot (klot)
contraction (kən trak′ shən)
export (v. eks pôrt′) (n. eks′ pôrt)
illustrate (il′ ə strāt)
intention (in ten′ shən)
orient (ôr′ ē ent)
pulse (puls)
seep (sēp)
vaccine (vak sēn′)

WORD STUDY

Prefixes

The prefix *mid-* means "in the middle of."

midair (mid âr′) not touching any surface
midnight (mid′ nīt) 12 o'clock at night
midsize (mid′sīz) the size between large and small
midterm (mid turm′) halfway though a period of schooling
midwinter (mid′ win′ tər) halfway through the coldest season
midyear (mid′ yēr) halfway through a 12-month period

Challenge Words

antagonize (an tag′ ə nīz)
baffle (baf′ əl)
confederate (kən fed′ ər it)
corrode (kə rōd′)
vain (vān)

WORDS IN CONTEXT

Read each sentence below to figure out the meaning of the word in **bold**. Use reasoning skills and the remainder of the sentence to help you. Write the meaning of the word on the line.

1. Christopher is so **sentimental** that he cries while looking at his old photos.

   _____

2. I noticed that water was beginning to **seep** through the crack in the pipe.

   _____

3. Sarah was taking a nap when an **unexpected** visitor knocked on the door.

   _____

4. **Vaccines** have wiped out many childhood diseases that were common only a few years ago.

   _____

5. Neil Armstrong was one of the first Americans to **explore** the moon's surface.

   _____

6. The two words *can* and *not* can be combined to form the **contraction** *can't*.

   _____

7. My hands were **numb** after I got caught outdoors in snowy weather without my gloves.

   _____

8. Before making her decision, the judge **contemplated** both sides of the issue.

   _____

9. I think it is an **insane** idea to dive into icy water in the middle of winter.

   _____

10. Thomas used a chart to **illustrate** how the accident happened.

   _____

WORD MEANINGS

Word Learning—Group A

Study the spelling, part(s) of speech, and meaning(s) of each word from Group A. Complete each sentence by writing the word on the line. Then read the sentence.

1. **acre** *(n.)* a unit of land equal to 43,560 square feet

   Each of the new houses will be built on an _____ of land.

2. **classify** *(v.)* to organize or arrange in groups or categories

   We plan to _____ these tree leaves and mount them in our science journals.

3. **contemplate** *(v.)* to think about or consider for a long time

   Before we panic, let's sit down and _____ the problem.

4. **explore** *(v.)* 1. to discover; 2. to investigate, study, or analyze

   Many people suffered great hardships in an effort to _____ the North Pole.

5. **ideal** *(n.)* 1. a standard of perfection; 2. a model to be imitated; 3. what one would want to be; *(adj.)* 1. existing as a mental image of perfection; 2. perfect

   Devin's dad is his _____.

   A week on a tropical island would be my _____ vacation.

6. **insane** *(adj.)* 1. crazy, mentally ill; 2. extremely foolish

   Climbing the tall tree to reach the window is an _____ idea.

7. **numb** *(adj.)* not having the power to feel or move normally; *(v.)* to dull the feelings of

   When Katherine first heard the news that her family would be moving, she was _____ with sadness.

   Before filling the tooth, the dentist will _____ your mouth.

8. **protein** *(n.)* a substance containing nitrogen that is a necessary part of animal and plant cells

   Paige suggested choosing a snack that is high in _____.

9. **sentimental** *(adj.)* 1. having or showing feeling; 2. acting from feelings rather than reason

   The old car is not worth much money, but it has _____ value for the whole family.

10. **unexpected** *(adj.)* 1. unforeseen; 2. surprising; 3. startling

    The _____ delay made us miss our next flight.

Use Your Vocabulary—Group A

Choose the word from Group A that best completes each sentence. Write the word on the line. You may use the plural form of nouns and the past tense of verbs if necessary.

For a long time, my pals and I __1__ what we would do during spring vacation. Then Cassidy suggested that we go hiking in a nearby national park. We could probably __2__ several __3__ of the park in just one day. At first, we thought her idea was __4__. It sounded too difficult and tiring to us. But the more we thought about it, the more __5__ the trip began to sound. We planned carefully, filling our packs with water and a variety of snacks that were high in __6__. Mom suggested that we take a first-aid kit, just in case something __7__ happened. But nothing bad did happen. We enjoyed spending the whole day outdoors, and we met a friendly ranger who helped us __8__ the plants and animals we had seen. We walked until our feet were __9__, but we really had fun. We still feel __10__ when we remember that day.

1. _____

2. _____

3. _____

4. _____

5. _____

6. _____

7. _____

8. _____

9. _____

10. _____

Vocabulary in Action

The word *vaccine* comes from the Latin word *vacca,* which means "cow." The first vaccine developed in the West was discovered by British physician Edward Jenner in 1796. Smallpox was a deadly disease that killed many people. Jenner discovered that people exposed to cowpox were immune to smallpox. Cowpox was similar to smallpox but weaker. Exposing people to cowpox made their bodies produce antibodies that protected them from smallpox. By 1977, vaccination programs such as those by the World Health Organization had eliminated smallpox worldwide.

Word Learning—Group B

Study the spelling, part(s) of speech, and meaning(s) of each word from Group B. Complete each sentence by writing the word on the line. Then read the sentence.

1. awkward *(adj.)* 1. clumsy; 2. lacking ease or grace when moving

Tristan hates parties because he thinks he is an _____ dancer.

2. clot *(n.)* a thick lump; *(v.)* to form into lumps

The leftover gravy formed _____ on the plate as it cooled.

The cut will stop bleeding as soon as the blood _____.

3. contraction *(n.)* 1. a drawing together; 2. a shortening or shrinking

The painful cramp in his leg was caused by a muscle _____.

4. export *(v.)* to send or carry goods out of one country for the use and sale in another; *(n.)* the act of carrying or removing something from a country

The United States hopes to _____ more goods in the future.

The _____ of native crafts is an important part of the small country's economy.

5. illustrate *(v.)* to make clear or explain by using stories or examples

Liam went on to _____ his answer with examples from his own experience.

6. intention *(n.)* 1. a plan of action; 2. a purpose

Malik has good _____, but something always goes wrong.

7. orient *(v.)* 1. to place something so it faces a particular direction; 2. to adjust to a new situation or environment

At first, Daisy found it difficult to _____ herself to the new school.

8. pulse *(n.)* any regular or measured beat or throb

The rapid _____ of the drums makes me feel like dancing.

9. seep *(v.)* to flow or pass slowly

When the heavy snow melted, water began to _____ through the roof.

10. vaccine *(n.)* a preparation of dead or weakened germs of a particular disease that is given to a person to prevent or lessen effects of that disease

Before starting school, most children are given a measles _____.

Use Your Vocabulary—Group B

Choose the word from Group B that best completes each sentence. Write the word on the line. You may use the plural form of nouns and the past tense of verbs if necessary.

Avery decided to spend her vacation learning to be a volunteer at the local hospital. Her day began with a tour to help her __1__ herself. Avery had many questions. She was afraid she might feel __2__ around sick people, so an experienced volunteer gave her examples that __3__ things she could say to patients. Avery comforted a child whose blood was beginning to __4__ through a bandage. She explained that the blood would soon __5__ and close the wound. She handed out juice to people who came in for their flu __6__, and a nurse showed her how to check the __7__ of a person's artery. She wheeled a patient who was having a painful muscle __8__ to the emergency room. At the end of the day, she toured the research lab, where chemists develop drugs that are __9__ all over the world. Avery was thrilled with the whole day. She made up her mind then and there that it was her __10__ to become a doctor.

1. _____

2. _____

3. _____

4. _____

5. _____

6. _____

7. _____

8. _____

9. _____

10. _____

 **SYNONYMS**

Synonyms are words that have the same or nearly the same meanings.

Part 1 Choose the word from the box that is the best synonym for each group of words. Write the word on the line.

insane	export	acre	classify	sentimental
pulse	protein	contraction	unexpected	ideal

1. shipping, sending from; transport   _____

2. sort, arrange, order   _____

3. reduction, shortening   _____

4. mad, lunatic, foolish _____

5. perfect, best, model _____

6. throb, regular beat, rhythm _____

7. important part of plant and animal cells _____

8. a measured amount of land _____

9. emotional, not based on reason _____

10. abrupt, surprising, sudden _____

Part 2 Replace the underlined word(s) with a word from the box that means the same or almost the same. Write your answer on the line.

contemplate	illustrate	clot	explore	awkward
numb	vaccine	seep	orient	intention

11. It is Aaliyah's <u>plan</u> to practice all summer to make the soccer team.

_____

12. Blood is liquid in your veins, but it will <u>solidify</u> when it is exposed to air.

_____

13. If you are exposed to a <u>weakened form of a disease</u>, you are less likely to contract the full form of the disease. _____

14. The committee will <u>look into</u> our ideas for a new teen center.

_____

15. Andy put ice on the injury to <u>dull</u> the pain. _____

16. Air began slowly to <u>leak</u> out of the punctured tire. _____

17. We used a compass to <u>locate</u> ourselves during the long hike.

_____

18. Aesop told stories to <u>give examples of</u> the lessons he taught.

_____

19. The newborn colt's first steps were shaky and <u>ungraceful</u>. _____

20. I promised to <u>ponder</u> my older sister's advice. _____

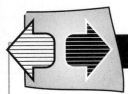

ANTONYMS

Antonyms are words that have opposite or nearly opposite meanings.

> ideal   insane   contraction   numb

Part 1 Choose the word from the box that is the best antonym for each group of words. Write the word on the line.

1. expansion, enlargement   _____

2. right-minded, not crazy   _____

3. sensitive, able to move   _____

4. common, ordinary, imperfect   _____

Part 2 Replace the underlined word(s) with a word from the box that means the opposite or almost the opposite. Write your answer on the line.

> sentimental   awkward   unexpected   contemplate

5. Giraffes move with <u>graceful</u> strides. _____

6. The council will probably <u>ignore</u> your comments. _____

7. The visit from Aunt Vickie was pretty <u>normal</u>. _____

8. As we threw away our old toys, we found ourselves being too <u>practical</u>.

_____

WORD STUDY

Prefixes Use the words in the box to write a sentence for each item.

> midair   midyear   midwinter
>
> midnight   midsize   midterm

1. Write about something that would be fun to do late at night.

_____

2. Write about something you might buy that is not the largest or the smallest.

_____

3. Write about the weather during the coldest part of the year.

_____

4. Write about something you do at school in the middle of the semester.

_____

5. Write about something you will be doing when this year is half over.

_____

6. Write about something that flies.

_____

CHALLENGE WORDS

Word Learning—Challenge!

Study the spelling, part(s) of speech, and meaning(s) of each word. Complete each sentence by writing the word on the line. Then read the sentence.

1. antagonize *(v.)* to create opposition or hostility

The fans' rude insults were meant to _____ the opposing team.

2. baffle *(v.)* 1. to bewilder; 2. to be too difficult for one to understand; 3. to confuse

Ciara's complicated ideas _____ her friends.

3. confederate *(n.)* 1. an ally; 2. an accomplice

Dante admitted that he was a _____ of the group who played the prank.

4. corrode *(v.)* to eat away slowly

Road salt will _____ your car's body if you don't wash it off quickly.

5. vain *(adj.)* 1. having too much pride in one's looks or ability; 2. conceited

The other students soon tired of listening to Tony's _____ boasts.

Use Your Vocabulary—Challenge!

My Spring Break Plan ahead for a way to enjoy your next school break. On a separate sheet of paper, write about an idea for having fun or for learning something new. Use the Challenge Words below.

| vain | antagonize | confederate | corrode | baffle |

FUN WITH WORDS

Start in the middle of the maze. Use a pencil to draw a line from each word to its definition. You may find more than one way to get to the definition.

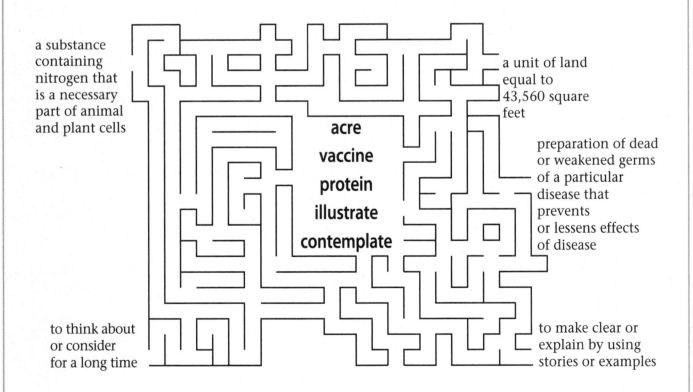

a substance containing nitrogen that is a necessary part of animal and plant cells

a unit of land equal to 43,560 square feet

acre

vaccine

protein

illustrate

contemplate

preparation of dead or weakened germs of a particular disease that prevents or lessens effects of disease

to think about or consider for a long time

to make clear or explain by using stories or examples

WORD LIST

Read each word using the pronunciation key.

Group A

adjust (ə just´)
coarse (kôrs)
convention (kən ven´ shən)

forbidding (fər bid´ iŋ)
imperfect (im pur´ fikt)
irrigation (ir ə gā´ shən)
legislator (lej´ is lāt ər)
oblige (ə blīj´)
shellac (shə lak´)
squeamish (skwēm´ ish)

Group B

administrator (əd min´ ə strāt ər)
compromise (kom´ prə mīz)
course (kôrs)
haggard (hag´ ərd)
irritate (ir´ ə tāt)
observe (əb zurv´)
ravine (rə vēn´)
sinister (sin´ is tər)
sterilize (stâr´ ə līz)
vault (vôlt)

WORD STUDY

Analogies

An analogy is a comparison between different things. Read and study the following analogies. Decide how the words in each analogy are related.

Sing is to **song** as **read** is to **story**.

Date is to **calendar** as **time** is to **clock**.

Rich is to **wealthy** as **ill** is to **sick**.

Challenge Words
deflect (di flekt´)
deteriorate (di tir´ ē ə rāt)
devastate (dev´ ə stāt)
diffuse (*adj.* di fyoos´) (*v.* di fyooz´)
dissension (di sen´ shən)

WORDS IN CONTEXT

Read each sentence below to figure out the meaning of the word in **bold**. Use reasoning skills and the remainder of the sentence to help you. Write the meaning of the word on the line.

1. After Nicholas put a coat of **shellac** on the old oak desk, it looked as good as new.

   _____

2. We sat quietly and **observed** the majestic bald eagles at the lake.

   _____

3. My brother **vaulted** over the fence and disappeared into the neighbor's yard.

   _____

4. The noise of the vacuum cleaner **irritates** the baby.

   _____

5. The **legislator** voted in favor of passing the new state law.

   _____

6. The race **course** follows the river to the top of the hill.

   _____

7. Alexis doesn't like that beach because the sand is too **coarse** and hurts her feet.

   _____

8. Dark, **sinister** clouds threatened rain during our picnic.

   _____

9. After being lost in the mountains for days, the pilot looked **haggard** but happy when he was rescued.

   _____

10. Natalie attended a national **convention** for student newspaper editors.

   _____

WORD MEANINGS

Word Learning—Group A

Study the spelling, part(s) of speech, and meaning(s) of each word from Group A.
Complete each sentence by writing the word on the line. Then read the sentence.

1. **adjust** *(v.)* 1. to adapt; 2. to become accustomed to

   It takes me about a week to _____ to daylight saving time.

2. **coarse** *(adj.)* 1. not fine; 2. rough

   The blanket is made of a _____ fabric that makes my skin itch.

3. **convention** *(n.)* an assembly of people meeting for some particular purpose

   José hoped he would be assigned to report on a political _____.

4. **forbidding** *(adj.)* 1. causing fear; 2. looking dangerous or unpleasant

   The growling polar bear looked so _____ I was glad there was a
   fence between us.

5. **imperfect** *(adj.)* not perfect; flawed

   Bryant's new glasses will correct his _____ vision.

6. **irrigation** *(n.)* a supplying of land with water

   In dry climates, farmers must build a system for _____ to water
   their crops.

7. **legislator** *(n.)* a member of a group that makes laws

   The voters' league keeps a record of how each _____ votes.

8. **oblige** *(v.)* 1. to make a person thankful or grateful; 2. to require; 3. to do a favor for

   Joining the club will _____ you to participate in at least three
   service projects.

9. **shellac** *(n.)* a type of varnish used as a wood filler and finish

   A sponge brush is a good tool for applying _____.

10. **squeamish** *(adj.)* easily sickened

    Shelby gets _____ whenever she is around animals.

Use Your Vocabulary—Group A

Choose the word from Group A that best completes each sentence. Write the word on the line. You may use the plural form of nouns and the past tense of verbs if necessary.

The life of a prospector was not for the __1__ . It took time to __2__ to the Wild West. Prospectors never held a(n) __3__ to get together and share ideas. It was every person for himself! Prospectors would climb even the most __4__ mountains if they thought they'd find gold there. They would look for land that showed signs of good __5__ . Then they would pan the __6__ sand in the streams to find gold nuggets. Even if they found some nuggets, __7__ ones weren't worth very much. Prospectors who staked a claim could put up a sign. They might even coat the sign with __8__ to keep the weather from washing off their name. But the prospectors had as much to fear from claim jumpers as the weather. The __9__ passed laws, but there was no one to enforce them. These daring adventurers were __10__ to look out for themselves.

1. _____

2. _____

3. _____

4. _____

5. _____

6. _____

7. _____

8. _____

9. _____

10. _____

Word Learning—Group B

Study the spelling, part(s) of speech, and meaning(s) of each word from Group B. Complete each sentence by writing the word on the line. Then read the sentence.

1. **administrator** *(n.)* a person who manages or directs

   The school _____ welcomed the students on the first day.

2. **compromise** *(v.)* to settle differences by agreeing that each side will give up part of what it demands

   Each group had to _____ to find a solution to the disagreement.

3. **course** *(n.)* 1. the route or direction taken by something; 2. a line of action; 3. a way of doing something; *(v.)* to flow quickly

   The sailor set a _____ toward home.

   The river's mighty waters _____ through the woods.

4. **haggard** *(adj.)* 1. looking worn, pale, and exhausted; 2. fatigued or worried

   We could tell by the firefighters' _____ faces that they had been battling the blaze all night.

5. **irritate** *(v.)* 1. to provoke impatience or anger; 2. to annoy

   Diana kept the speech short so as not to _____ the audience.

6. **observe** *(v.)* 1. to watch; 2. to notice; 3. to show regard for

   Jalen and Jody often use a telescope to _____ the night sky.

7. **ravine** *(n.)* a long, deep, narrow valley usually worn down by running water

   Rocks and tree roots stuck out from both sides of the _____.

8. **sinister** *(adj.)* 1. threatening; 2. evil; 3. dishonest

   The villain of the play had a _____ grin.

9. **sterilize** *(v.)* to free from living germs

   Before we preserve the fruit, Mom must _____ the jars.

10. **vault** *(v.)* to jump or leap over something using some kind of support, such as a pole or the hands

    After spotting the bull, Kaleb hurried to _____ over the fence.

Use Your Vocabulary—Group B

Choose the word from Group B that best completes each sentence. Write the word on the line. You may use the plural form of nouns and the past tense of verbs if necessary.

Some pioneers went west in search of land, not gold. They often went in wagon trains with a leader who acted as __1__. If the settlers looked __2__ at the end of their journey, it was because they faced many obstacles along their __3__. It was hard to get huge, clumsy wagons through deep __4__, and a team of oxen could not just __5__ over a mountain. Water might have to be __6__ before the thirsty travelers could take a drink. Sometimes a(n) __7__ person caused trouble on a wagon train. But usually trouble started because people were __8__ by traveling closely together for a long time. A wise leader __9__ the group very carefully. If he was able to head off trouble by suggesting acceptable __10__, the travelers made it safely to their new homes.

1. _____

2. _____

3. _____

4. _____

5. _____

6. _____

7. _____

8. _____

9. _____

10. _____

 **SYNONYMS**

Synonyms are words that have the same or nearly the same meanings.

Part 1 Choose the word from the box that is the best synonym for each group of words. Write the word on the line.

observe	shellac	imperfect	squeamish	irritate
coarse	legislator	sinister	irrigation	haggard

1. easily ill, sensitive, delicate _____

2. harmful, menacing, unkind _____

3. notice, watch; celebrate _____

4. lawmaker, member of government _____

5. annoy, bother, pester _____

6. tired-looking, weary, gaunt _____

7. flawed, defective, unsound _____

8. rough, scratchy, prickly _____

9. the watering of land _____

10. varnish, polish _____

Part 2 Replace the underlined word(s) with a word from the box that means the same or almost the same. Write your answer on the line.

forbidding	course	adjust	sterilize	vault
oblige	compromise	convention	ravine	administrator

11. Brook tries to <u>accommodate</u> her friends when they ask for a favor.

_____

12. Edgar's python looks <u>frightening</u>, but he is very gentle. _____

13. The caravan stayed on <u>the route</u> during the blizzard. _____

14. The couple agreed to <u>meet halfway</u> to settle their quarrel. _____

15. We learned a lot at the baseball card collectors' <u>conference</u>. _____

16. Geni found it hard to <u>adapt</u> to playing in the new league. _____

17. After each patient, the dentist must <u>disinfect</u> her instruments.

_____

18. The muddy donkey climbed up the side of the <u>gorge</u>. _____

19. Every gymnast must learn to <u>spring</u> over the horse. _____

20. The workers took their complaints to the <u>manager</u>. _____

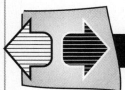 **ANTONYMS**

Antonyms are words that have opposite or nearly opposite meanings.

Part 1 Choose the word from the box that is the best antonym for each group of words. Write the word on the line.

squeamish	ravine	forbidding	compromise	observe

1. neglect, pay no attention to _____

2. mountain, peak _____

3. quarrel, contest, disagree _____

4. inviting, welcoming, pleasant _____

5. not easily upset or sickened _____

> ## Vocabulary in Action
>
> The word **sinister** comes from a Latin word that means "on the left" or "unlucky." For many centuries, people who used their left hands were discouraged from doing so. Right-handed people were the majority, and they thought there was something wrong or unnatural about people who were left-handed. Luckily for left-handed people everywhere, this isn't the case in most of the world today. There are many examples of famous lefties—Benjamin Franklin, Bill Clinton, Helen Keller, Charlie Chaplin, Marie Curie, and Joan of Arc, to name just a few. Left-handers even have their own day. International Left-Handers Day is August 13.

Level E   Chapter 6

Part 2 Replace the underlined word with a word from the box that means the opposite or almost the opposite. Write your answer on the line.

imperfect	coarse	sinister	irritated	haggard

6. The loud music from Chance's stereo <u>calmed</u> his mother. _____

7. Genesis looked <u>lively</u> the morning after her trip. _____

8. The painting is a <u>flawless</u> example of the Dutch style. _____

9. The cheetah leaped to its feet and gave a <u>harmless</u> growl. _____

10. The <u>smooth</u> wool sweater is warm but scratchy. _____

WORD STUDY

Analogies Select the word that completes each analogy.

1. **Color** is to **red** as **shape** is to _____.
   - (a.) scissors
   - (b.) blue
   - (c.) square
   - (d.) arithmetic

2. **Word** is to **book** as **ingredient** is to _____.
   - (a.) cook
   - (b.) recipe
   - (c.) mix
   - (d.) letter

3. **Attempt** is to **try** as **avoid** is to _____.
   - (a.) escape
   - (b.) awaken
   - (c.) greet
   - (d.) tempt

4. **Call** is to **shout** as **build** is to _____.
   - (a.) construct
   - (b.) demolish
   - (c.) telephone
   - (d.) hammer

5. **Morning** is to **afternoon** as **breakfast** is to _____.
   - (a.) eat
   - (b.) evening
   - (c.) cereal
   - (d.) lunch

6. **Foot** is to **ankle** as **hand** is to _____.

a. toe

c. wrist

b. finger

d. shake

CHALLENGE WORDS

Word Learning—Challenge!

Study the spelling, part(s) of speech, and meaning(s) of each word. Complete each sentence by writing the word on the line. Then read the sentence.

1. **deflect** *(v.)* to turn aside

   Josue put up his hand to _____ the snowball Elizabeth threw.

2. **deteriorate** *(v.)* to become worse in quality or value

   These cheap shoes began to _____ the first time I wore them.

3. **devastate** *(v.)* 1. to destroy; 2. to overwhelm

   A tornado can _____ a whole town in just a few minutes.

4. **diffuse** *(adj.)* 1. not concentrated; 2. scattered; *(v.)* to spread out

   By the time we got there, the smoke was so _____ you could barely see it anymore.

   The farmer made sure to _____ seeds to all parts of the field.

5. **dissension** *(n.)* 1. disagreement; 2. continuous quarreling

   The umpire's call caused _____ between the two teams.

Use Your Vocabulary—Challenge!

Time Machine Of all the periods in our world's history, which one would you like to have lived in? Think about what life was like during that era and what you would be doing. On a separate sheet of paper, report on what you might see in that era. Use the Challenge Words above.

FUN WITH WORDS

Use the clues to complete the puzzle. Choose from the words listed below. You will not use all the words.

compromise	ravine	oblige	convention	sinister
sterilize	shellac	squeamish	adjust	haggard
irritate	imperfect	course	observe	vault

Across

2. to settle an argument by agreeing that each side give up part of what it demands
6. to leap over something using a pole or hands
7. a long, deep, narrow valley usually worn by running water
8. threatening; evil
9. to watch and take note

Down

1. to annoy
2. an assembly of people arranged for a particular purpose
3. made to feel sick easily
4. not perfect
5. to free from living germs
9. to do a favor for

Review 4–6

Word Meanings Fill in the bubble of the word that is best defined by each phrase.

1. to clear up
   - a. consist
   - b. explore
   - c. clarify
   - d. export

2. a plan of action
   - a. scheme
   - b. progress
   - c. protein
   - d. pulse

3. one time every year
   - a. annual
   - b. unexpected
   - c. numb
   - d. coarse

4. something that is a bother
   - a. atmosphere
   - b. injection
   - c. acre
   - d. nuisance

5. looking tired and worn out
   - a. awkward
   - b. sinister
   - c. haggard
   - d. squeamish

6. damaged, faulty
   - a. imperfect
   - b. nimble
   - c. classic
   - d. orient

7. scary, dangerous-looking
   - a. triumphant
   - b. forbidding
   - c. irritate
   - d. imperfect

8. absolutely perfect
   - a. insane
   - b. awkward
   - c. ideal
   - d. numb

9. to study carefully
   - a. contemplate
   - b. clot
   - c. encounter
   - d. compromise

10. to find out about
    - a. classify
    - b. explore
    - c. consist
    - d. illustrate

11. to mix together
    - a. sterilize
    - b. prompt
    - c. acquire
    - d. homogenize

12. to ooze
    - a. acquaint
    - b. seep
    - c. encounter
    - d. clot

13. to urge into action without delay
    - a. oblige
    - b. clarify
    - c. consist
    - d. prompt

14. the way something goes
    - a. coarse
    - b. scheme
    - c. course
    - d. security

15. out of the ordinary
    - a. uncivilized
    - b. sentimental
    - c. annual
    - d. exceptional

Sentence Completion
Choose the word from Part 1 that best completes each of the following sentences. Write the word in the blank. Then do the same for Part 2. You will not use all the words.

Part 1

awkward	exceptional	prompted	conscience
acquire	observe	vaulted	orient

1. The _____ boy ran across the yard and crashed into a chair.

2. Cecilia ran down the field, placed the pole, and _____ ten meters up into the air.

3. _____ the plants so that they face the sun.

4. Let's pack a picnic and _____ the fireworks display.

5. My _____ told me I should not keep the wallet I found.

Part 2

acres	administrator	ravine	irrigation
export	adjust	vaccine	pulse

6. We're going to _____ this new computer game to countries around the world.

7. The pounding rain washed dirt and small rocks into the _____.

8. They drove across Kansas and passed _____ of golden grain.

9. We've only lived here for two weeks, so I have not had time to _____ to my new school.

10. Fifty years ago, everyone in the group was given a(n) _____ to prevent smallpox.

Synonyms
Synonyms are words that have the same or nearly the same meanings. Choose the word from the box that is the best synonym for each group of words. Write your answer on the line.

unexpected	illustrate	irrigation	sterilize	nimble
security	clot	progress	oblige	

1. the watering of land   _____

2. mass, clump; solidify, thicken   _____

3. move on, growth   _____

4. disinfect, purify, clean   _____

5. abrupt, surprising, sudden   _____

6. safety, protection, safeguard   _____

7. spry, agile, graceful   _____

8. give examples, clear up   _____

9. accommodate, help   _____

Antonyms
Antonyms are words that have opposite or nearly opposite meanings. Choose the word from the box that is the best antonym for each group of words. Write your answer on the line.

sentimental	insane	squeamish	contraction	encounter
compromise	irritate	classic	uncivilized	

1. right-minded, not crazy   _____

2. not easily upset or sickened   _____

3. work of no value, of poor quality   _____

4. avoid, escape, retreat   _____

5. calm, ease, comfort   _____

6. expansion, enlargement   _____

7. quarrel, contest, disagree   _____

8. reasonable, realistic, practical _____

9. refined, educated, settled _____

Word Riddles Choose the word from the box that answers the riddle. Write it on the line.

| administrator | injection | classify | triumphant |
| sinister | convention | acquire | intention |

1. I am a verb.

I am what you do when you sort laundry.
I am a synonym of *arrange*.

I am _____.

2. I am a noun.

I begin with a prefix and end with a suffix.
I mean "a gathering of people meeting for a purpose."

I am _____.

3. I am a noun.

I am something you plan to do.
I hope yours is good!

I am _____.

4. I am a noun.

I am the person in charge.
I am a synonym of *director*.

I am _____.

5. I am a verb.

I rhyme with *desire*.
I am what you do when you get something.

I am _____.

6. I am an adjective.

I rhyme with *minister*.
But I am evil and menacing.

I am _____.

7. I am a noun.

You may not want me, but I'm good for you.
I end in a suffix.

I am _____.

8. I am an adjective.

I am the way you feel when you are successful.
I am an antonym of *defeated*.

I am _____.

CHAPTER 7

WORD LIST

Read each word using the pronunciation key.

Group A

absolute (ab sə lo͞ot´)
abundant (ə bun´ dənt)
admirable (ad´ mər ə bəl)
criticize (krit´ i sīz)
frame (frām)
impure (im pyo͝or´)
issue (ish´ yo͞o)
recall (*v.* ri kôl´) (*n.* rē´ kôl)
stern (stərn)
vertebra (vər´ tə brə)

Group B

aggressive (ə gres´ iv)
boast (bōst)
comment (kom´ ent)
cultivate (kul´ tə vāt)
fraud (frôd)
incident (in´ si dənt)
kerosene (ker´ ə sēn)
reclaim (ri klām´)
strive (strīv)
victorious (vik tôr ē əs)

WORD STUDY

Suffixes

The suffix *-ship* means "a state or quality of being" or "the art or skill of."

authorship (ô´ thər ship) the profession of a writer
championship (cham´ pyən ship) a game or contest that determines an overall winner
friendship (frend´ ship) an amicable relationship
kinship (kin´ ship) the connection between family members
scholarship (skol´ ər ship) knowledge attained by studying
sportsmanship (spôrts´ mən ship) fair and honest behavior

Challenge Words

expenditure (ik spen´ di chər)
fastidious (fa stid´ ē əs)
gaudy (gô´ dē)
humility (hyo͞o mil´ i tē)
paltry (pôl´ trē)

WORDS IN CONTEXT

Read each sentence below to figure out the meaning of the word in **bold.** Use reasoning skills and the remainder of the sentence to help you. Write the meaning of the word on the line.

1. The **stern** expression on my mother's face let me know she was angry because I was late.

   _____

2. We remembered to bring **kerosene** for our camp stove, but we forgot the matches.

   _____

3. Divers went down to see whether the ancient shipwreck could be **reclaimed.**

   _____

4. Andrew's friends soon tired of listening to him **boast** about his new bike.

   _____

5. Her face was familiar, but I could not **recall** her name.

   _____

6. The **victorious** tennis team held a party to celebrate winning the tournament.

   _____

7. Afterward, we realized we should not have **criticized** Hailey's decision to quit the basketball team.

   _____

8. Dr. Hunter's claim that his potion could make people fly was discovered to be a **fraud.**

   _____

9. "Our company," declared the president, "will continue to **strive** to find new ways to improve our service."

   _____

10. Melissa did not want her **comments** to be misunderstood, so she took the time to explain herself carefully.

   _____

WORD MEANINGS

Word Learning—Group A

Study the spelling, part(s) of speech, and meaning(s) of each word from Group A. Complete each sentence by writing the word on the line. Then read the sentence.

1. **absolute** *(adj.)* 1. complete; 2. not limited in any way

   Before testifying, Cole swore to tell the _____ truth.

2. **abundant** *(adj.)* more than enough

   The settlers prepared an _____ supply of food for the winter.

3. **admirable** *(adj.)* 1. worth admiring; 2. very good; 3. excellent

   Jorge has so many _____ talents.

4. **criticize** *(v.)* 1. to find fault with; 2. to consider the good and bad points of something and judge accordingly

   After the movie, my friends and I gathered to _____ it.

5. **frame** *(v.)* 1. to lie to make an innocent person appear guilty; 2. to shape; 3. to construct; *(n.)* something composed of parts fitted together

   The accused man said that others wanted to _____ him.

   The builders began by putting up the _____ of the house.

6. **impure** *(adj.)* 1. not pure; 2. mixed with something of a lesser value

   That ring is inexpensive because it is made of _____ gold.

7. **issue** *(v.)* 1. to send out; 2. to put forth; *(n.)* a matter that is in dispute between two or more people

   The police chief promised to _____ a statement about the arrest.

   The students asked the counselor to help them settle the _____.

8. **recall** *(v.)* 1. to call back to mind; 2. to remember; *(n.)* a call to return something

   It's fun to _____ the good times we had last summer.

   The car manufacturer issued a _____ because some of the air bags were slow to inflate.

9. **stern** *(adj.)* severe; strict; harsh

   The general is a fair but _____ leader.

10. **vertebra** *(n.)* one of the bones that makes up the backbone

    Veronica fractured a _____ when she fell from her skateboard.

Use Your Vocabulary—Group A

Choose the word from Group A that best completes each sentence. Write the word on the line. You may use the plural form of nouns and the past tense of verbs if necessary.

For 50 years, Preston had bought every stamp __1__ by the post office. He had a(n) __2__ collection. His __3__ supply of stamps filled his whole house, and Preston could easily __4__ every stamp he owned. One day Preston came home and discovered that the glass case he had once __5__ to protect his most valuable stamp was unlocked. He was filled with complete and __6__ terror. The stamp was gone! He heard a creak, and every muscle along each __7__ of his back tightened. Preston called out, "Halt!" in a(n) __8__ voice. He raced down the hall and saw a figure limp quickly away. Suddenly Preston felt like his invaded home was dirty and __9__ . His hand shook as he dialed the police. At that moment, no one would have __10__ Preston for his angry thought: "I hope that rotten thief gets what he deserves!"

1. _____

2. _____

3. _____

4. _____

5. _____

6. _____

7. _____

8. _____

9. _____

10. _____

Word Learning—Group B

Study the spelling, part(s) of speech, and meaning(s) of each word from Group B. Complete each sentence by writing the word on the line. Then read the sentence.

1. **aggressive** *(adj.)* 1. making the first move in an attack or a quarrel; 2. attacking

   Slowly back away from an _____ alligator.

2. **boast** *(v.)* to speak of oneself or what one owns with excessive pride

   Ashlyn tried not to _____ about her new car too often.

3. **comment** *(n.)* a note or remark expressing opinion or attitude; *(v.)* to make a note or remark

   Trenton was cheered by the coach's encouraging _____.

   The reporter invited people to _____ on the new law.

4. **cultivate** *(v.)* 1. to help plants grow by working and caring for them; 2. to improve by labor, care, or study

   It takes lots of hard work to _____ a rose garden.

5. **fraud** (*n.*) 1. someone who is not what he or she pretends to be; 2. deception

   The investigator gathered enough evidence to expose the _____.

6. **incident** (*n.*) 1. a happening or an occurrence; 2. something dependent on something of greater importance

   Because of the _____ in the gym, two players were suspended.

7. **kerosene** (*n.*) a thin oil made from petroleum and used as fuel for lamps, stoves, and engines

   We lit the cabin with lamps that burned _____.

8. **reclaim** (*v.*) 1. to bring back to a useful, good condition; 2. to rescue from an undesirable state

   We can _____ this overgrown garden with hard work.

9. **strive** (*v.*) to work or try hard

   Jed promised that he would _____ to improve his grades.

10. **victorious** (*adj.*) 1. having won a victory; 2. of or relating to victory; 3. successful

    The crowd stood and cheered for the _____ athlete.

Use Your Vocabulary—Group B

Choose the word from Group B that best completes each sentence. Write the word on the line. You may use the plural form of nouns and the past tense of verbs if necessary.

Police Sergeant Conner answered the call. He listened without __1__ to Preston's story and then said, "I hate to __2__, but in my 20 years, I have solved every case." Sergeant Conner promised to __3__ to solve this case too. From the beginning, he took a(n) __4__ approach. He __5__ his interest in stamps. After he had learned all he could, he read the new police reports. He read about a(n) __6__ in which a suspicious character posing as a stamp expert had tried to sell a rare stamp to a stamp dealer. Sergeant Conner arranged to be at the shop the next day. He had the dealer pretend the power had failed and lit __7__ lamps. Then Conner hid in the shadows. When the thief came in, the sergeant shouted, "I arrest you for __8__!" He __9__ Preston's stamp and was __10__ once again.

1. _____

2. _____

3. _____

4. _____

5. _____

6. _____

7. _____

8. _____

9. _____

10. _____

SYNONYMS

Synonyms are words that have the same or nearly the same meanings.

Part 1 Choose the word from the box that is the best synonym for each group of words. Write the word on the line.

issue	recall	reclaim	admirable	incident
absolute	criticize	impure	aggressive	vertebra

1. remember; a request to give back   _____

2. hostile, bold, charging   _____

3. unclean, not filtered   _____

4. judge, not approve of   _____

5. distribute, give out; problem, dispute   _____

6. episode, event, occasion   _____

7. wonderful, worthy of praise   _____

8. total, thorough, whole   _____

9. a bone in the back   _____

10. take back, restore, recover   _____

Vocabulary in Action

Vertebra comes from the Latin word *vertere*, which means "to turn." Other words that come from this word include *verse, vertigo, introvert,* and *anniversary.* Find these words in a dictionary. Do you see how each word includes some kind of "turn"?

Part 2 Replace the underlined word with a word from the box that means the same or almost the same. Write your answer on the line.

fraud	kerosene	comments	boast	strive
stern	frame	abundant	cultivate	victorious

11. Abraham made a few very smart <u>observations</u> about the novel.

_____

12. The <u>structure</u> of the new house will be made of steel, not wood.

_____

13. The swindler is going to jail for committing a <u>deception</u>. _____

14. We ask only that you always <u>attempt</u> to play your best chess game.

_____

15. We lit the <u>oil</u> in our antique lamps. _____

16. Mallory earns excellent grades, but she does not <u>brag</u> about them.

_____

17. The sergeant's <u>tough</u> words stirred the soldiers to action. _____

18. The farmer began to <u>plant</u> her crops in early spring. _____

19. The <u>triumphant</u> hockey team will take home the trophy. _____

20. A <u>plentiful</u> feast was prepared for the workers. _____

ANTONYMS

Antonyms are words that have opposite or nearly opposite meanings.

Part 1 Choose the word from the box that is the best antonym for each group of words. Write the word on the line.

strive	fraud	victorious
reclaim	stern	abundant

1. truth, good faith, honesty _____

2. destroy, make unusable _____

3. goof off, be lazy _____

4. insufficient, scarce, not enough _____

5. defeated, beaten, overcome _____

6. permissive, soft, easygoing _____

Part 2 Replace the underlined word(s) with a word from the box that means the opposite or almost the opposite. Write your answer on the line.

aggressive	criticize	recall
impure	admirable	issue

7. The board member took time to <u>praise</u> the new policy. _____

8. The police officer said he had to <u>take back</u> a ticket. _____

9. We felt light-headed after breathing all that <u>wholesome</u> air. _____

10. I can't seem to <u>forget</u> my awful first experience at summer camp.

    _____

11. Pierce spent the weekend engaged in <u>terrible</u> activities. _____

12. Daron is too <u>shy</u> to be successful as a sales representative. _____

WORD STUDY

Suffixes Read each story. Write the word from the box that names the story's theme.

friendship	scholarship	kinship
championship	authorship	sportsmanship

1. With two outs in the last inning, the Eagles were ahead by one run. Yesenia pitched a high fastball. Crack! A home run. It was all over for the Eagles. Yesenia felt like crying, but she forced herself to smile as she passed the opponent's bench. "Congratulations," she said. "You played a great game!"

   _____

2. Every morning, Zackary goes into his office and turns on the computer. Even if he's tired or has a bad day, he forces himself to write at least one page of his novel. One day, he will see his novel on the library shelf.

   _____

3. Albert and Fabian like to spend time together. When Fabian is sad, Albert cheers him up. When Fabian gets something new, he can't wait to share it with Albert. They hope their relationship will last forever.

   _____

4. Each year the Washington family holds a reunion. Babies are introduced, and the families share stories. Cousins remember how much fun it is to be together. All the Washingtons value their time together.

_____

5. Kassandra spends lots of time studying. She is the first member of her family to go to college. Her grades put her at the top of her class. She studies hard not only to keep up her grades. She knows that if she studies hard enough, she can find an alternative to gasoline and change the world.

_____

6. Tabitha has competed in a dozen chess tournaments. This year, though, she is the second-ranked player in her division. She has spent the entire weekend playing against her opponents. She has defeated all the lower-ranked players. There is only one player left to beat. He is the top-ranked player. Tabitha plans to take home that trophy this year, and Devonte Charles is not going to stop her!

_____

CHALLENGE WORDS

Word Learning—Challenge!

Study the spelling, part(s) of speech, and meaning(s) of each word. Complete each sentence by writing the word on the line. Then read the sentence.

1. **expenditure** (*n.*) 1. spending; 2. the amount of time, energy, or money spent

   Ramon realized that another _____ was not in his budget.

2. **fastidious** (*adj.*) 1. difficult to please; 2. fussy or picky

   Gina is _____ about the placement of every object in her room.

3. **gaudy** (*adj.*) cheap; showy; tasteless

   I liked the outfit, but Shaun said it was too _____.

4. **humility** (*n.*) 1. lack of arrogance; 2. meekness

   _____ is an appealing quality in a star athlete.

5. **paltry** (*adj.*) almost worthless

   Viviana thought the job was worth more than that _____ sum.

Use Your Vocabulary—Challenge!

It's a Mystery Do you think you would make a good detective? On a separate sheet of paper, try writing a mystery story for practice. Tell about the crime and the solution. Use the Challenge Words below.

> expenditure   fastidious   gaudy   humility   paltry

 FUN WITH WORDS

An *anagram* is a word made by mixing up the letters of one word in order to spell another word. For example, rearranging the letters of the word *moat* gives us the anagram *atom*. The letters are the same; they're just in a different order.

In the challenge below, you'll see an equation like this:

Example: seeker + no = an oily seeker _____

The letters to the left of the equal sign are an anagram of a vocabulary word (plus one or two additional letters that are needed to complete the word). The words to the right of the equal sign give you a hint. In the sample above, combine the letters from the word *seeker* with the letters *no* and rearrange them. You should come up with *kerosene*, a word that describes a type of oil. Write the vocabulary word in the blank.

1. bats + o = you can brag about your bats _____

2. rent + s = this rent is very serious _____

3. prime + u = this anagram should be cleaned _____

4. earl + lc = do you remember this earl? _____

5. moment + c = at this moment, I must speak _____

6. camel + ir = I want my camel back! _____

7. rebate + vr = watch your back on this one _____

8. tables + ou = truly complete tables _____

9. lattice + uv = make this lattice grow _____

10. alarmed + ib = this is an excellent alarm _____

CHAPTER 8

 WORD LIST

Read each word using the pronunciation key.

Group A

alarm (ə lärm´)
buff (buf)
common (kom´ ən)
frontier (frun tēr´)
incidental (in si den´ təl)
legend (lej´ ənd)
manacle (man´ ə kəl)
orbit (ôr´ bit)
reduce (ri dōōs´)
vivid (viv´ id)

Group B

bureau (byŏŏr´ ō)
commotion (kə mō´ shən)
deliberately (di lib´ ər it lē)
genuine (jen´ yŏŏ in)
inconsiderate (in kən sid´ ər it)
magnificent (mag nif´ i sənt)
parasite (pâr´ ə sīt)
reign (rān)
suppress (sə pres´)
survey (sər vā´)

 WORD STUDY

Root Words

The root *scribe* means "write."

ascribe (ə skrīb´) to credit to; to attribute to

describe (di skrīb´) to tell or write about

inscribe (in skrīb´) to write a person's name on a list; to write a short message in a book

prescribe (prē skrīb´) to write an order for medicine; to give advice

proscribe (prō skrīb´) to forbid

subscribe (səb skrīb´) to sign an agreement for a product or service; to give approval to

Challenge Words

brusque (brusk)
dexterity (dek ster´ i tē)
incessant (in ses´ ənt)
peerless (pēr´ lis)
pompous (pom´ pəs)

Level E

WORDS IN CONTEXT

Read each sentence below to figure out the meaning of the word in **bold**. Use reasoning skills and the remainder of the sentence to help you. Write the meaning of the word on the line.

1. This summer I plan to **reduce** the amount of time I spend watching TV.

   _____

2. The sheriff placed a **manacle** on the prisoner's wrists to prevent his escape.

   _____

3. It's obvious that Jessica did not **deliberately** break the glass.

   _____

4. The **reign** of the beloved queen continued for many years.

   _____

5. The smoke from Joseph's science experiment set off the fire **alarm**.

   _____

6. Alexandra tried to **suppress** her urge to giggle during her sister's recital.

   _____

7. Jordan loves to wax the car, and she will **buff** it over and over until it gleams.

   _____

8. As the satellite follows its **orbit** around the earth, it sends back valuable weather information.

   _____

9. Everyone was delighted by the food at the **magnificent** banquet.

   _____

10. The museum curator proved that the newly found painting was a **genuine** work by Picasso.

    _____

WORD MEANINGS

Word Learning—Group A

Study the spelling, part(s) of speech, and meaning(s) of each word. Complete each sentence by writing the word on the line. Then read the sentence.

1. **alarm** *(v.)* to make afraid or frighten; *(n.)* 1. sudden fear; 2. a signal that warns people

   "I don't mean to _____ you," Jackson said, "but you are about to sit on a bumblebee."

   The class formed an orderly line at the sound of the fire _____.

2. **buff** *(v.)* to polish or shine; *(n.)* soft, orange-yellow leather used for polishing

   Ask someone at the auto body shop to _____ out that scratch on your fender.

   Ian carefully polished the car with a clean, new _____.

3. **common** *(adj.)* 1. general; 2. usual; 3. having no special position; 4. belonging to all in a group

   All the members of the chess club shared a _____ interest.

4. **frontier** *(n.)* 1. the last edge of developed country; 2. a border between countries

   Life on the _____ held many hardships for the pioneers.

5. **incidental** *(adj.)* occurring by chance

   The two friends were pleased by their _____ meeting.

6. **legend** *(n.)* 1. a story coming down from the past that may or may not be based on fact; 2. an explanatory list of symbols on a chart

   The story of Paul Bunyan is an American folk _____.

7. **manacle** *(n.)* something used to bind or secure a wrist; a handcuff

   The prisoner was secured by a _____ on each arm.

8. **orbit** *(n.)* the circular path of an object around another object, usually in space

   Earth travels in an _____ around the sun.

9. **reduce** *(v.)* 1. to make smaller; 2. to decrease

   Every day Kaylee tries to _____ the amount of time it takes her to run a mile.

10. **vivid** *(adj.)* 1. having the appearance of freshness; 2. in colors, very strong

    The _____ colors of the sunset were reflected in the lake.

Use Your Vocabulary—Group A

Choose the word from Group A that best completes each sentence. Write the word on the line. You may use the plural form of nouns and the past tense of verbs if necessary.

Oral historians travel around the country collecting old songs and __1__ . Some of the best can be traced back to the pioneers who settled the western __2__ . According to one story, attacks by bandits and wild animals were so __3__ that the pioneers didn't even blink when it happened. But even the bravest pioneer was __4__ by the thought of an attack by the ferocious half-bear, half-horse beast called Krakakatoe. To __5__ the possibility of a surprise attack, the settlers hired Big Dallas Dawes to protect them. One night Dallas stayed up late to __6__ his new sheriff's badge. As he walked out into the moonlight to see if the badge was shiny enough, he had a(n) __7__ meeting with the slobbering, howling Krakakatoe. Dazzled by the bright glare of the badge, the monster stopped short. Dallas quickly attached a(n) __8__ to the monster's wrist and tied his lasso to it. Then he swung the rope—and the monster—above his head and hurled it clear into __9__ . And the monster is there still. Have you ever heard a(n) __10__ howl in the night? That's the Krakakatoe flying overhead.

1. _____

2. _____

3. _____

4. _____

5. _____

6. _____

7. _____

8. _____

9. _____

10. _____

Vocabulary in Action

The word *manacle* has the same Latin root as several other English words including *manifest* and *emancipate*. Its Latin root *manus* means "hand." The word *manacle* first appeared around the year 1306.

Word Learning—Group B

Study the spelling, part(s) of speech, and meaning(s) of each word from Group B. Complete each sentence by writing the word on the line. Then read the sentence.

1. **bureau** *(n.)* 1. a chest of drawers, sometimes with a mirror; 2. a division of a government department

    Mom folded the T-shirts and placed them in a drawer in the baby's

    _____.

2. **commotion** *(n.)* 1. a violent movement; 2. confusion; 3. disturbance

    A cougar caused a _____ at the barbecue.

3. **deliberately** *(adv.)* 1. on purpose; 2. after careful and thorough consideration

    Mikayla explained that she had not picked up the wrong backpack

    _____.

4. **genuine** *(adj.)* 1. actual; 2. true; 3. sincere; 4. honest

    It appears that the party was a _____ surprise to Ariana.

5. **inconsiderate** *(adj.)* careless of others and their feelings, thoughtless

    Margaret apologized for making an _____ remark that hurt Edward's feelings.

6. **magnificent** *(adj.)* grand; splendid; impressive

    Isabelle wore _____ jewelry to the dance.

7. **parasite** *(n.)* a living thing that spends its life on or in another, which it usually injures

    Because the tree had been invaded by some kind of _____, we had to cut it down.

8. **reign** *(n.)* the period of power of a ruler; royal authority; *(v.)* to rule

    The _____ of Henry VIII was filled with scandals.

    Erik already knew he was next in line to _____ over his country.

9. **suppress** *(v.)* 1. to put an end to; 2. to hold in or back; 3. to stop with force

    Troops were sent to the town to _____ the rebellion.

10. **survey** *(v.)* 1. to examine; 2. to inspect

    The president flew over the area in a helicopter to _____ the flood damage.

Use Your Vocabulary—Group B

Choose the word from Group B that best completes each sentence. Write the word on the line. You may use the plural form of nouns and the past tense of verbs if necessary.

An international research team, sent to __1__ a remote region of Mochea, made an important discovery. Among the ancient ruins, the team found a statue of a Royal Mountain leech, an extinct __2__ that disappeared hundreds of years ago. The researchers thought that the statue was an artifact from the __3__ of Queen Xalia, the greatest ruler of ancient Mochea. With its gold casting and brilliant colors, the statue was a valuable and __4__ piece of art. The researchers shipped the statue to the International __5__ of Ancient Civilizations for further study. When it arrived, the golden leech created quite a(n) __6__ among the experts. Thorough testing confirmed that the statue was indeed __7__. The researchers were thrilled. They wanted to claim the statue, but the Mochean government asked that it be returned. At first, some members of the team planned to __8__ ignore the request. But they soon realized that they had to __9__ their dishonest and __10__ desires for history's sake. Today the statue is back in the country that has been its home for hundreds of years.

1. _____

2. _____

3. _____

4. _____

5. _____

6. _____

7. _____

8. _____

9. _____

10. _____

 **SYNONYMS**

Synonyms are words that have the same or nearly the same meanings.

Part 1 Choose the word from the box that is the best synonym for each group of words. Write the word on the line.

alarm	frontier	deliberately	reduce	magnificent
inconsiderate	incidental	suppress	parasite	genuine

1. rude, thoughtless, insensitive _____

2. purposefully, in an unhurried way _____

3. real, authentic, proven, pure   _____

4. scare, panic; alert, fear   _____

5. lessen, shrink, diminish   _____

6. overcome, stop, smother   _____

7. edge, boundary   _____

8. wonderful, fine, superb   _____

9. thing that lives in or on another   _____

10. unplanned, accidental   _____

Part 2 Replace the underlined word(s) with a word from the box that means the same or almost the same. Write your answer on the line.

| orbit | vivid | buff | reign | commotion |
| survey | legend | manacle | bureau | common |

11. The community members worked toward a <u>public</u> goal. _____

12. <u>Look over</u> the headings and questions before you read. _____

13. The slave broke the <u>shackle</u> and escaped to freedom. _____

14. The engineers sighed with relief as the satellite settled into its <u>pathway around the earth.</u> _____

15. The antique <u>cabinet</u> filled one whole wall of the room. _____

16. It's fun to sit around a campfire and tell an <u>old story.</u> _____

17. The arrival of the movie star caused an <u>uproar</u> at the mall. _____

18. Mercedes had to <u>polish</u> her shoes until her face was reflected in them.

_____

19. The <u>bright</u> colors in the painting attracted my attention. _____

20. The new queen promised to <u>govern</u> with kindness and fairness.

_____

ANTONYMS

Antonyms are words that have opposite or nearly opposite meanings.

Part 1 Choose the word from the box that is the best antonym for each group of words. Write the word on the line.

deliberately	commotion	common
suppress	incidental	vivid

1. continue, express, let out   _____

2. peace, calm, quiet   _____

3. dull, colorless, pale   _____

4. impulsively, suddenly, quickly   _____

5. not usual, private, secret   _____

6. planned, occurring on purpose   _____

Part 2 Replace the underlined word(s) with a word from the box that means the opposite or almost the opposite. Write your answer on the line.

genuine	reduce	alarmed
magnificent	frontier	inconsiderate

7. I liked Lindsay right away because of her <u>insincere</u> smile. _____

8. We were <u>calmed</u> when we heard the TV weather bulletin. _____

9. The family planned to build a new life in the <u>settled region</u>.

     _____

10. It's a good idea to <u>increase</u> the amount of sugar in our diet.

     _____

11. We all gathered on the porch to gaze at the <u>ordinary</u> rainbow.

     _____

12. The other children found Sergio's comments <u>thoughtful</u>. _____

WORD STUDY

Root Words Add a prefix from the box to the root to make a word that fits each clue. Then write a sentence using the word.

> a-   de-   in-   pre-   pro-   sub-

1. An action that is forbidden by law is _____ scribed.

   _____

2. A rumor can be _____ scribed to the person who began it.

   _____

3. You can sign a contract to _____ scribe to your favorite magazine.

   _____

4. A doctor may _____ scribe medicine to treat an illness.

   _____

5. Before you give a book as a gift, you may want to _____ scribe a message on the inside front cover.

   _____

6. A person who told what something looks like has _____ scribed it.

   _____

CHALLENGE WORDS

Word Learning—Challenge!

Study the spelling, part(s) of speech, and meaning(s) of each word. Complete each sentence by writing the word on the line. Then read the sentence.

1. **brusque** *(adj.)* 1. abrupt; 2. blunt

   Calvin's _____ answer discouraged the reporter from asking any more questions.

2. **dexterity** *(n.)* skill and ease in using the hands, mind, or body

   April handles her skateboard with amazing _____.

3. incessant *(adj.)* continuing without interruption

The child's _____ snoring kept the whole family awake.

4. peerless *(adj.)* 1. without a match; 2. without an equal

The _____ skater won the gold medal easily.

5. pompous *(adj.)* 1. arrogant; 2. acting too proudly

The audience walked out on the _____ and long-winded speaker.

Use Your Vocabulary—Challenge!

Tell the Tale Stories such as the legend of Krakakatoe are called tall tales. American pioneers told tall tales around a campfire after a day of grueling travel. What other tall tales do you know? On a separate sheet of paper, create a new tall tale that describes another adventure Big Dallas Dawes might have had. Use the Challenge Words below.

| brusque | dexterity | incessant | peerless | pompous |

FUN WITH WORDS

King Ragnama wants you to join the quest for the Golden Dictionary. But first you must pass a final test to prove your worthiness. Answer each of King Ragnama's questions below.

1. Name two things that *alarm* you.

   _____

2. Name one *genuine* act of kindness you have performed recently.

   _____

3. Describe the most *magnificent* thing you have ever seen.

   _____

4. Parts of the kingdom are not yet settled. Would you be willing to journey to the *frontier*? Why or why not?

   _____

5. Would you agree to travel with an *inconsiderate* but very strong person? Why or why not?

   _____

WORD LIST

Read each word using the pronunciation key.

Group A

caravan (kâr´ ə van)
competition (kom pi tish´ ən)
destination (des tə nā´ shən)
indigo (in´ də gō)
magnify (mag´ nə fī)
mutual (myo͞o´ cho͞o əl)
parliament (pär´ lə mənt)
relate (ri lāt´)
survival (sər vī´ vəl)
wedge (wej)

Group B

cell (sel)
compensation (kom pən sā´ shən)
completion (kəm plē´ shən)
disassemble (dis ə sem´ bəl)
greedily (grēd´ i lē)
industry (in´ də strē)
remedy (rem´ i dē)
revolt (ri vōlt´)
tactics (tak´ tiks)
yearn (yərn)

WORD STUDY

Prefixes

The prefix *sub-* means "under."

subfreezing (sub frē´ ziŋ) below a temperature of 32° Fahrenheit
submarine (sub´ mə rēn) something that lives or operates underwater
submerge (səb mərj´) to place underwater
subsoil (sub´ soil) the layer of dirt under the topsoil
substandard (sub stan´ dərd) inferior to or different from the norm
subway (sub´ wā) an underground passage or railway

Challenge Words

confirm (kən fərm´)
conflict (*n.* kon´ flikt) (*v.* kən flikt´)
defer (di fər´)
precipitate (pri sip´ i tāt)
steep (stēp)

WORDS IN CONTEXT

Read each sentence below to figure out the meaning of the word in **bold.** Use reasoning skills and the remainder of the sentence to help you. Write the meaning of the word on the line.

1. Taylor offered Daniel 10 dollars as **compensation** for mowing her lawn.

_____

2. At the bonfire, Savannah **related** stories about her travels in Mongolia.

_____

3. The unhappy peasants united to plan a **revolt** against the wicked king.

_____

4. Kyle **greedily** ate all the best snacks before the guests arrived.

_____

5. After the photo had been **magnified,** the detective was able to spot a clue that helped her solve the mystery.

_____

6. As soon as the concert ended, workers began to **disassemble** the portable stage.

_____

7. Freezing temperatures and hungry polar bears make **survival** in the Arctic very difficult.

_____

8. Tactics such as whining and crying will not make Christina change her mind.

_____

9. As soon as the Andersons reach their **destination,** they plan to check in, change, and jump into the swimming pool.

_____

10. Garrett and Kelly have a **mutual** interest in punk rock records.

_____

WORD MEANINGS

Word Learning—Group A

Study the spelling, part(s) of speech, and meaning(s) of each word from Group A. Complete each sentence by writing the word on the line. Then read the sentence.

1. **caravan** *(n.)* a group of people traveling together, often through dangerous areas

   As the _____ headed west, the onlookers cheered and waved.

2. **competition** *(n.)* 1. the act of two or more people independently trying to win or gain something; 2. a contest

   Unfortunately, the tennis _____ was postponed due to rain.

3. **destination** *(n.)* the place a person or thing is being sent

   Be sure to leave early enough to reach your _____ on time.

4. **indigo** *(n.)* a blue dye that can be obtained from various plants

   Before making the shawl, Riley colored her yarn with _____.

5. **magnify** *(v.)* to cause objects to appear larger than they really are

   We had to _____ the bacteria with the microscope before we were able to see them.

6. **mutual** *(adj.)* 1. having similar or shared feelings; 2. given and received

   By _____ agreement, Alexis and Summer decided to never quarrel again.

7. **parliament** *(n.)* the highest lawmaking body in some countries

   Nolan hopes to be elected to _____ someday.

8. **relate** *(v.)* 1. to give an account of; 2. to tell; 3. to show a connection between

   Josiah was invited to _____ stories of his childhood.

9. **survival** *(n.)* 1. the act of surviving; 2. living or continuing longer than others

   The _____ of a species depends upon its ability to change over time.

10. **wedge** *(n.)* a piece of wood or metal that tapers to a thin edge

   Marco placed a _____ under the door to keep it from closing.

Use Your Vocabulary—Group A

Choose the word from Group A that best completes each sentence. Write the word on the line. You may use the plural form of nouns and the past tense of verbs if necessary.

Would you like me to __1__ the story of our class trip? The __2__ was Ottawa, the capital of Canada. Our __3__ of three buses started out while it was still dark. The sky looked as if it had been dyed with __4__. As the sun rose, we spotted a flock of geese. They were flying in a formation shaped like a(n) __5__ and were heading the same way we were. We were all wide awake, so we decided to have a singing __6__. Each side of the bus tried to drown out the other. Finally, our teachers begged us to stop. They claimed it was life or death, a matter of __7__, but you know how teachers are. They seem to __8__ every little thing. In Ottawa, we had lunch and then watched members of __9__ at work. By the time we climbed back in the buses to go home, we were almost as tired as our teachers. By __10__ agreement, we decided to sleep all the way home.

1. _____

2. _____

3. _____

4. _____

5. _____

6. _____

7. _____

8. _____

9. _____

10. _____

Word Learning—Group B

Study the spelling, part(s) of speech, and meaning(s) of each word from Group B. Complete each sentence by writing the word on the line. Then read the sentence.

1. **cell** (*n.*) extremely small unit of living matter that makes up all living things

    In biology class, we identified the parts of a plant _____.

2. **compensation** (*n.*) 1. something given to someone to make up for something else; 2. an equivalent; 3. pay

    Peyton didn't want _____ for his volunteer work.

3. **completion** (*n.*) 1. finishing; 2. the act of being finished or done

    The school will celebrate the _____ of the new library.

4. **disassemble** (*v.*) to take apart

    The historical society plans to _____ the old log cabin and rebuild it in the city park.

5. **greedily** (*adv.*) acting with a strong desire to have a lot of something

    As the guests arrived, Ava _____ grabbed each present.

6. **industry** *(n.)* 1. all such business, manufacture, and trade taken as a whole; 2. manufacturing as a whole; 3. steady effort

    Adrianna plans to train for a career in the automotive _____.

7. **remedy** *(v.)* to cure; *(n.)* a treatment that relieves or cures a disease

    My plan will _____ the crowding problems in the lunchroom.

    Six patients volunteered to test the new cold _____.

8. **revolt** *(n.)* the act of rebelling; *(v.)* to turn and fight against a leader

    The _____ of the colonists led to the birth of the United States.

    The tyrant didn't think his subjects would _____ against him.

9. **tactics** *(n.)* 1. ways or methods to gain advantage; 2. ways to accomplish an end

    The president approved of General Clark's _____.

10. **yearn** *(v.)* 1. to feel a longing or desire; 2. to feel tenderness

    A month of snowy days made Lauren _____ for summer.

Use Your Vocabulary—Group B

Choose the word from Group B that best completes each sentence. Write the word on the line. You may use the plural form of nouns and the past tense of verbs if necessary.

When I took the babysitting job, I expected to spend a quiet evening studying for my biology test on __1__ while little Trey slept. Instead I had to cope with a preschooler who was in __2__. Trey was as destructive as the whole demolition __3__ put together. First, he tried to __4__ the TV remote control. When I turned my back, he broke into a "childproof" cabinet and __5__ ate a whole box of cookies. No matter what __6__ I tried, I couldn't seem to __7__ the situation. It wasn't long before I was beginning to __8__ for the job's __9__. I swore that no amount of __10__ would make me sit for Trey ever again. But then little Trey crawled into my lap. "You're my favorite babysitter," he said sweetly. Maybe I will try it one more time.

1. _____

2. _____

3. _____

4. _____

5. _____

6. _____

7. _____

8. _____

9. _____

10. _____

SYNONYMS

Synonyms are words that have the same or nearly the same meanings.

Part 1 Choose the word from the box that is the best synonym for each group of words. Write the word on the line.

yearn	indigo	destination	wedge	parliament
compensation	remedy	disassemble	relate	survival

1. heal, treat; cure, medicine   _____

2. want, long for, desire   _____

3. living, staying alive, lasting   _____

4. target, goal, journey's end   _____

5. dismantle, take down, break up   _____

6. pie-shaped piece of wood or metal   _____

7. reward, fee, payback   _____

8. lawmaking body   _____

9. blue dye   _____

10. report, speak, tell   _____

Part 2 Replace the underlined word(s) with a word from the box that means the same or almost the same. Write your answer on the line.

cell	greedily	competition	mutual	completion
caravan	tactics	industry	revolt	magnify

11. Tatiana and Elise became friends because of their <u>shared</u> interests.

   _____

12. The <u>procession</u> of trucks formed a long line on the highway. _____

13. Members of the computer <u>business</u> attended a convention. _____

14. The <u>rebellion</u> ended when the dictator fled the country. _____

15. If we <u>enlarge</u> the picture, we might see our faces in the crowd.

   _____

Chapter 9   Level E

© Loyola Press.

16. Some creatures only have one <u>living unit of matter</u>. _____

17. Allen used underhanded <u>methods</u> to convince people to give him their money. _____

18. We cheered as our ferret won the ugly pet <u>contest</u> at the fair. _____

19. The baby birds chirped <u>hungrily</u> in the nest. _____

20. If you pass the class, you will receive a certificate of <u>finishing</u>.

_____

 **ANTONYMS**

Antonyms are words that have opposite or nearly opposite meanings.

Part 1 Choose the word from the box that is the best antonym for each group of words. Write the word on the line.

survival	revolt	magnify
mutual	compensation	completion

1. cause to look smaller _____

2. death, extermination, extinction _____

3. loss, expense _____

4. starting, beginning _____

5. one-sided, separate _____

6. obey, give loyalty to; support _____

Vocabulary in Action

The word *magnify* first appeared in the English language around 1380. At that time, it meant "to praise" or "to speak of the glory of something or someone." In older translations of the Bible, you can still find the phrase "magnify the Lord." This doesn't mean "to make God bigger." The meaning of the word has changed. *Magnify* first meant "to cause objects to appear larger than they really are" around 1665, almost 300 years after the word surfaced in English.

Part 2 Replace the underlined word(s) with a word from the box that means the opposite or almost the opposite. Write your answer on the line.

yearn	remedy	disassemble
destination	relate	competition

7. The doctor prescribed a <u>poison</u> to treat the disease. ⎯⎯⎯⎯⎯⎯

8. The hikers reached their <u>starting point</u> by sunset. ⎯⎯⎯⎯⎯⎯

9. The <u>cooperation</u> between the candidates was incredible. ⎯⎯⎯⎯⎯⎯

10. Saul had to <u>build</u> a car engine before he could understand how it worked.

   ⎯⎯⎯⎯⎯⎯

11. Her long travels on boats and trains made Miranda <u>hate</u> to sleep at home again.

   ⎯⎯⎯⎯⎯⎯

12. My older sister loves to <u>keep secret</u> tales of my childhood. ⎯⎯⎯⎯⎯⎯

WORD STUDY

Prefixes Use two words from the box to answer each question.

submarine	subfreezing	submerge
subsoil	substandard	subway

1. What might happen if a contractor built a building on a patch of ground with an underground stream running through it?

   ⎯⎯⎯⎯⎯⎯⎯⎯⎯⎯⎯⎯⎯⎯⎯⎯⎯⎯⎯⎯⎯

2. What might happen if a criminal tried to dispose of a weapon by throwing it into a pond when the temperature has been below 32° Fahrenheit for a month?

   ⎯⎯⎯⎯⎯⎯⎯⎯⎯⎯⎯⎯⎯⎯⎯⎯⎯⎯⎯⎯⎯

3. What is the difference between a ride in a vehicle that travels underwater and a ride in a vehicle that travels underground?

   ⎯⎯⎯⎯⎯⎯⎯⎯⎯⎯⎯⎯⎯⎯⎯⎯⎯⎯⎯⎯⎯

CHALLENGE WORDS

Word Learning—Challenge!

Study the spelling, part(s) of speech, and meaning(s) of each word. Complete each sentence by writing the word on the line. Then read the sentence.

1. confirm *(v.)* 1. to prove true; 2. to give approval

The scientists planned a series of experiments that would finally either

_____ or disprove their theory.

2. conflict *(n.)* 1. a fight; 2. lack of agreement; *(v.)* to strongly disagree

The _____ began with a misunderstanding.

Ryan's opinions _____ with those of Paola.

3. defer *(v.)* 1. to put off; 2. to postpone; 3. to give in to an opinion

Ezekiel had to _____ his vacation until the busy season was over.

4. precipitate *(v.)* 1. to bring about abruptly; 2. to condense as water vapor that then falls in the form of rain or snow

The confusion over the boundary may _____ a crisis between the two countries.

5. steep *(adj.)* having a sharp angle or slope; *(v.)* to soak in a liquid

Waves crashed against the _____ cliff.

Before cooking the meat, Linda will _____ it overnight in her special sauce.

Use Your Vocabulary—Challenge!

All in a Day's Work Have you ever had a babysitting job or another type of job? What was hard about it? What was fun? On a separate sheet of paper, write about a job you have had or would like to have. Use the Challenge Words above.

FUN WITH WORDS

You have found the Golden Dictionary of Spelrix! You must discover the secret phrase that will unlock the book. Match the vocabulary words with the definitions below. Write one letter of the word in each blank. Use the numbered letters to find out the secret phrase at the bottom of the page, and the Golden Dictionary will be yours!

1. ways to accomplish an end ___ ___ ___ ___ ___ ___ ___
                              1

2. continuing longer than others ___ ___ ___ ___ ___ ___ ___ ___
                                2

3. a treatment for a disease ___ ___ ___ ___ ___ ___
                            3

4. to make something appear larger ___ ___ ___ ___ ___ ___ ___
                                  4

5. a lawmaking body ___ ___ ___ ___ ___ ___ ___ ___ ___
                   5

6. acting with a desire to have a lot ___ ___ ___ ___ ___ ___ ___ ___
                                    6

7. all of manufacturing ___ ___ ___ ___ ___ ___ ___ ___
                        7

8. money received for work ___ ___ ___ ___ ___ ___ ___ ___ ___ ___ ___
                          8

9. to long for ___ ___ ___ ___ ___
              9

10. a V-shaped piece of wood ___ ___ ___ ___ ___
                             10

11. having feelings that are alike ___ ___ ___ ___ ___ ___
                                  11

12. a blue dye ___ ___ ___ ___ ___ ___
               12

Secret phrase: ___ ___ ___ ___ ___ ___   ___ _H_ ___ ___ ___ ___
               11 6 10 11 9 8   1   12 12 8 5

___ ___ ___ ___   ___ ___ ___ ___ ___   ___ ___ ___ ___ ___ ___ .
 9 12 2 7   10 12 7 3 8   10 4 8 5 6 9

Review 7–9

Word Meanings Fill in the bubble of the word that is best defined by each phrase.

1. true and sincere
   - (a.) incidental
   - (b.) genuine
   - (c.) abundant
   - (d.) aggressive

2. a group of lawmakers
   - (a.) parliament
   - (b.) revolt
   - (c.) frontier
   - (d.) industry

3. to make useful again
   - (a.) suppress
   - (b.) caravan
   - (c.) reclaim
   - (d.) manacle

4. a list that explains symbols on a map or chart
   - (a.) incident
   - (b.) fraud
   - (c.) bureau
   - (d.) legend

5. an oil used as fuel
   - (a.) kerosene
   - (b.) cell
   - (c.) parasite
   - (d.) orbit

6. to show how one thing connects to another
   - (a.) yearn
   - (b.) relate
   - (c.) strive
   - (d.) issue

7. a blue dye made from certain plants
   - (a.) remedy
   - (b.) vertebra
   - (c.) indigo
   - (d.) compensation

8. to shrink
   - (a.) buff
   - (b.) recall
   - (c.) reclaim
   - (d.) reduce

9. strict and hard
   - (a.) inconsiderate
   - (b.) aggressive
   - (c.) stern
   - (d.) impure

10. ways to get something
    - (a.) destination
    - (b.) tactics
    - (c.) comment
    - (d.) survival

11. to study carefully
    - (a.) survey
    - (b.) cultivate
    - (c.) revolt
    - (d.) criticize

12. a backbone
    - (a.) vertebra
    - (b.) indigo
    - (c.) wedge
    - (d.) competition

13. done or said after careful thought
    - (a.) deliberately
    - (b.) mutual
    - (c.) greedily
    - (d.) genuine

14. to make a steady effort
    - (a.) frame
    - (b.) strive
    - (c.) disassemble
    - (d.) cultivate

15. very brightly colored
    - (a.) admirable
    - (b.) common
    - (c.) vivid
    - (d.) victorious

Sentence Completion Choose the word from Part 1 that best completes each of the following sentences. Write the word in the blank. Then do the same for Part 2. You will not use all the words.

Part 1

alarm	commotion	bureau	mutual
remedy	suppress	frame	absolute

1. Allie built the _____ of the birdhouse first.

2. Cara decided that only the _____ quiet of the library would help her concentrate.

3. Let's not _____ the citizens with crazy rumors.

4. The people causing all the _____ outside made Guillermo look up from his book.

5. The doctor has just found a(n) _____ for the patient's mysterious illness.

Part 2

wedge	revolt	magnify	common
reign	completion	magnificent	comment

6. The audience cheered wildly at the _____ display of fireworks.

7. Elian whittled the block of wood until he had made a _____ for the door.

8. The critic praised the new play, but he made a negative _____ about the silly costumes.

9. The young king did his best to _____ over his subjects firmly but fairly.

10. Scientists used a microscope to _____ the red blood cells and make them visible to the eye.

Synonyms

Synonyms Synonyms are words that have the same or nearly the same meanings. Choose the word from the box that is the best synonym for each group of words. Write your answer on the line.

abundant	buff	competition	caravan	orbit
revolt	common	cultivate	incident	

1. course, pathway, circuit   _____

2. rebellion; mutiny, rise up against   _____

3. plant, farm, develop, nurture   _____

4. ordinary, plain, public   _____

5. episode, event, occasion   _____

6. match, contest   _____

7. plentiful, more than enough   _____

8. rub, brighten; a type of leather   _____

9. band, procession, fleet   _____

Antonyms

Antonyms Antonyms are words that have opposite or nearly opposite meanings. Choose the word from the box that is the best antonym for each group of words. Write your answer on the line.

completion	victorious	recall	survival	impure
incidental	frontier	mutual	aggressive	

1. death, extermination, extinction   _____

2. interior, settled region   _____

3. defeated, beaten, overcome   _____

4. planned, occurring on purpose   _____

5. peaceful, shy, friendly   _____

6. clean, wholesome, unpolluted   _____

7. forget, not remember   _____

8. one-sided, separate _____

9. starting, beginning _____

Word Riddles Answer each riddle with a word from the box. Write the word on the line.

cell	yearn	bureau	fraud
inconsiderate	greedily	boast	disassemble

1. I am a noun.
I am a piece of furniture.
I am a synonym of *cabinet*.

I am _____.

2. I am an adjective.
I describe a rude person.
I begin with a prefix.

I am _____.

3. I am a verb.
I mean "to break down or take apart."
I am an antonym of *build*.

I am _____.

4. I am a noun.
I am a part of every living thing.
I rhyme with *well*.

I am _____.

5. I am a verb.
I am a habit others get tired of hearing.
I am a synonym of *brag*.

I am _____.

6. I am a verb.
I mean "to want badly or long for."
I rhyme with *turn*.

I am _____.

7. I am a noun.
I am a dishonest person or scheme.
I am a synonym of *cheating*.

I am _____.

8. I am an adverb.
I can describe the way a person eats.
I am an antonym of *unselfishly*.

I am _____.

Review 7–9   Level E

Posttest

Choosing the Definitions

Fill in the bubble next to the item that best defines the word in bold in each sentence.

1. The late nineteenth century was an era of great westward **migration.**
   - (a.) direction
   - (b.) view
   - (c.) movement
   - (d.) retreat

2. From the top of the mountain, we could **survey** the scene below.
   - (a.) inspect
   - (b.) enjoy
   - (c.) paint
   - (d.) organize

3. Fill out your application and give it to the program **administrator.**
   - (a.) office
   - (b.) participant
   - (c.) director
   - (d.) helper

4. The king's army was surprised by the sudden **revolt.**
   - (a.) loud noise
   - (b.) trembling
   - (c.) uprising
   - (d.) illness

5. After a delay at the beginning, we **progressed** rapidly.
   - (a.) finished
   - (b.) advanced
   - (c.) stopped
   - (d.) delivered

6. Austin used a toy to **distract** the baby from pulling on the lamp cord.
   - (a.) divert
   - (b.) punish
   - (c.) annoy
   - (d.) teach

7. Ethan didn't realize that his hurtful **comment** was heard at the next table.
   - (a.) grip
   - (b.) remark
   - (c.) exercise
   - (d.) song

8. Maybe reading the movie's review will **prompt** Victoria to come with us.
   - (a.) demand
   - (b.) challenge
   - (c.) forbid
   - (d.) encourage

9. Rachel is in charge of **circulation** for the school newspaper.
   - (a.) sending around
   - (b.) editing
   - (c.) writing
   - (d.) folding

10. Anna was delighted by the chance **encounter** with her old friend.
    - (a.) call
    - (b.) meeting
    - (c.) gift
    - (d.) illness

11. "We need to make some new rules about the **uncivilized** behavior in the lunchroom," Sydney declared.
    - (a.) proper
    - (b.) odd
    - (c.) wild
    - (d.) annoying

12. Destiny tried to **suppress** a yawn during the boring program.
    - (a.) smother
    - (b.) let out
    - (c.) sleep
    - (d.) allow

13. Our new car came with a one-year **guarantee.**
    - (a.) plan
    - (b.) promise
    - (c.) trip
    - (d.) delay

14. The captain depended on lighted buoys to help him pass through the **channel** at night.
    - (a.) darkness
    - (b.) light mist
    - (c.) doorway
    - (d.) deep water

15. Noah always felt **sentimental** when he thought of his old neighborhood.
    a. angry   **b.** emotional   **c.** unhappy   **d.** abandoned

16. Morgan said the new boy was handsome, but I thought he had a **sinister** grin.
    a. threatening   **b.** ugly   **c.** childish   **d.** wide

17. Jonathan hoped the dentist would not find any cavities during his **routine** checkup.
    a. rare   **b.** boring   **c.** regular   **d.** canceled

18. The **ravine** in our backyard makes a good hiding place.
    a. valley   **b.** playhouse   **c.** oak   **d.** hill

19. Every so often, I like to find a quiet spot and **contemplate** life.
    a. forget about   **b.** reflect on   **c.** remember   **d.** pursue

20. For Christian, an **ideal** vacation is a week on the ski slopes.
    a. ruined   **b.** relaxing   **c.** perfect   **d.** free

21. Jennifer won first prize for her **exceptional** painting.
    a. colorful   **b.** modern   **c.** strange   **d.** outstanding

22. On our field trip to the museum, we saw many **classic** works of art.
    a. modern   **b.** colorful   **c.** excellent   **d.** interesting

23. It is impossible to ride a bicycle on this rocky **terrain**.
    a. land   **b.** roadway   **c.** journey   **d.** shore

24. Some **legends** were created to explain things people did not understand.
    a. lectures   **b.** old stories   **c.** formulas   **d.** paintings

25. Only groups with guides were allowed to use the **perilous** hiking trail.
    a. risky   **b.** scenic   **c.** expensive   **d.** natural

26. Jasmine moved slowly and **deliberately** toward the roaring dragon.
    a. swiftly   **b.** timidly   **c.** purposefully   **d.** carelessly

27. Haley turned down the job because she felt that the **compensation** was not adequate.
    a. workplace   **b.** title   **c.** hours   **d.** pay

28. Rebecca listened carefully to the astrologer's **prediction**.
    a. song   **b.** foretelling   **c.** tale   **d.** memory

29. Dylan was a good nurse because he treated his patients with **compassion**.
    a. rudeness   **b.** skill   **c.** kindness   **d.** coolness

30. Stephanie had a **novel** idea for her science project.
    a. unusual   **b.** dangerous   **c.** boring   **d.** difficult

Word Relations

Synonyms are words that have the same or nearly the same meanings. Antonyms are words that have opposite or nearly opposite meanings.

In the blank before each pair of words, write *S* if the words are synonyms, *A* if they are antonyms, or *N* if they are not related.

1. _____	protein	pulse	16. _____	mercy	compassion
2. _____	accumulate	molecule	17. _____	parasite	vertebra
3. _____	inconsiderate	respectful	18. _____	clarify	complicate
4. _____	irritate	annoy	19. _____	triumphant	victorious
5. _____	traitor	treaty	20. _____	coarse	numb
6. _____	incidental	unexpected	21. _____	sinister	forbidding
7. _____	inherent	victorious	22. _____	imperfect	ideal
8. _____	abolish	preserve	23. _____	circumference	cell
9. _____	fraud	common	24. _____	bureau	debris
10. _____	scheme	tactic	25. _____	common	mutual
11. _____	clarify	illustrate	26. _____	imperfect	impure
12. _____	orbit	injection	27. _____	legislator	infantry
13. _____	issue	frame	28. _____	magnify	reduce
14. _____	compliment	criticize	29. _____	parliament	theory
15. _____	caravan	abandon	30. _____	ambition	intention

Using Context Clues

Use the word in bold and the sentence context to underline the phrase that best completes each sentence.

1. A **wedge** is useful as a
   - **a.** ladder.
   - **b.** saw.
   - **c.** doorstop.
   - **d.** chair.

2. If you go to a **convention**, you will probably
   - **a.** spend a lot of time alone.
   - **b.** meet many new people.
   - **c.** invent something useful.
   - **d.** see classic words of art.

3. If you like to **harmonize**, you like to
   - a. carry a tune.
   - b. make up after a quarrel.
   - c. tell jokes.
   - d. bake fancy desserts.

4. If someone speaks of her distant **destination**, she may be referring to
   - a. a relative.
   - b. her dentist.
   - c. her favorite star.
   - d. her travel plans.

5. The man accused of murder was **framed**; he was
   - a. made to look guilty.
   - b. photographed.
   - c. famous.
   - d. frightened.

6. If you sound **hoarse**, you might have a
   - a. toothache.
   - b. sore throat.
   - c. pony.
   - d. fear of speaking in public.

7. Maria rented a **furnished** apartment because she didn't have any
   - a. food.
   - b. time.
   - c. carpeting.
   - d. furniture.

8. The nineteenth **century** lasted
   - a. one hundred years.
   - b. nineteen years.
   - c. nineteen months.
   - d. one hundred days.

9. If you have a **contraction** in your muscle, your muscle probably feels
   - a. relaxed.
   - b. itchy.
   - c. cramped.
   - d. warm.

10. If you can **relate** apples to oranges, you can
    - a. show how they are different.
    - b. set them next to each other.
    - c. do a magic trick.
    - d. show how they are the same.

11. When the queen's **reign** ended, she
    - a. put away her umbrella.
    - b. shouted "Bravo!"
    - c. lost her power.
    - d. lost her memory.

12. A person whose hobby is **vaulting** probably
    - a. likes to fly through the air.
    - b. likes to go underground.
    - c. is afraid of heights.
    - d. enjoys the water.

13. Todd felt a bit **squeamish** as he
- a. listened to the soft music.
- b. drifted off to sleep.
- c. chewed his favorite gum.
- d. watched the horror movie.

14. Upon her **completion** of the bike race, Sophia felt
- a. ashamed that she dropped out.
- b. proud that she finished.
- c. worried about her flat tire.
- d. afraid she'd never make it.

15. If you buy an **imperfect** pair of shoes, they may
- a. not fit.
- b. last a long time.
- c. feel great.
- d. look great.

16. **Testimony** is often given
- a. at a party.
- b. in outer space.
- c. in a court of law.
- d. in a hospital.

17. **Pneumonia** is a disease that affects
- a. farm animals.
- b. the lungs.
- c. the spine.
- d. houseplants.

18. If you could ride in a **satellite**, you would be
- a. under the ground.
- b. in the water.
- c. in outer space.
- d. on a railroad track.

19. People who **boast**
- a. love snowy weather.
- b. brag about things they own.
- c. are modest about their talents.
- d. are usually very good cooks.

20. You may get a **vaccine**
- a. in a doctor's office.
- b. on a tropical island.
- c. in an appliance store.
- d. in an apartment building.

21. To care for a **guppy**, you must
- a. take it for walks.
- b. teach it to fetch.
- c. brush it every day.
- d. change its water.

22. A coat of **shellac**
- a. can keep you warm.
- b. is made of fur.
- c. can be put on a table.
- d. is usually called a jacket.

23. A person wearing a **manacle** probably

   (**a.**) is wealthy.   (**c.**) has poor vision.

   (**b.**) is a prisoner.   (**d.**) is a child.

24. Someone who eats **greedily**

   (**a.**) is eating everything in sight.   (**c.**) only eats dessert.

   (**b.**) is using good manners.   (**d.**) is a very picky eater.

25. If you are **awkward**,

   (**a.**) you would make a good dancer.   (**c.**) you would make a good athlete.

   (**b.**) you are very intelligent.   (**d.**) you often bump into things.

26. An **annual** event

   (**a.**) takes place once a month.   (**c.**) takes place every year.

   (**b.**) takes place in the city.   (**d.**) takes place in a park.

27. If you make an **appeal**, you

   (**a.**) cook a fruit pie.   (**c.**) will use a sewing machine.

   (**b.**) ask for help.   (**d.**) donate some money.

28. Farmers use an **irrigation** system to

   (**a.**) plow their fields.   (**c.**) feed their animals.

   (**b.**) harvest their crops.   (**d.**) water their crops.

29. An **aggressive** dog

   (**a.**) may attack as you walk by.   (**c.**) will run if you come near it.

   (**b.**) has won a prize at a dog show.   (**d.**) never barks at strangers.

30. A person who is a **nuisance**

   (**a.**) is fun to be around.   (**c.**) is an annoying pest.

   (**b.**) has a lot of money.   (**d.**) has just moved next door.

Test-Taking Tips

Taking a standardized test can be difficult. Here are a few things you can do to make the experience easier.

Get a good night's sleep the night before the test. You want to be alert and rested in the morning.

Eat a healthful breakfast. Your brain needs good food to work properly.

Wear layers of clothing. You can take off or put on a layer if you get too warm or too cold.

Bring two sharp number 2 pencils with erasers.

When you get the test, read the directions carefully. Be sure you understand what you are supposed to do. If you have any questions, ask your teacher before you start marking your answers.

If you feel nervous, close your eyes and take a deep breath as you silently count to three. Then slowly breathe out. Do this several times until your mind is calm.

Manage your time. Check to see how many questions there are. Try to answer half the questions before half the time is up.

Answer the easy questions first. If you don't know the answer to a question, skip it and come back to it later if you have time.

Try to answer all the questions. Some will seem very hard, but don't worry about it. Nobody is expected to get every answer right. Make the best guess you can.

If you make a mistake, erase it completely. Then write the correct answer or fill in the correct circle.

When you have finished, go back over the test. Work on any questions you skipped. Check your answers.

Question Types

Many tests contain the same kinds of questions. Here are a few of the question types that you may encounter.

Meaning from Context

This kind of question asks you to figure out the meaning of a word from the words or sentences around it.

The smoke from the smoldering garbage made her eyes water.

Which word in the sentence helps you understand the meaning of *smoldering*?

smoke garbage
eyes water

Read the sentence carefully. You know that smoke comes from something that is burning. *Smoldering* must mean "burning." *Smoke* is the correct answer.

Synonyms and Antonyms

Some questions ask you to identify the synonym of a word. Synonyms are words that have the same or nearly the same meaning. Some questions ask you to identify the antonym of a word. Antonyms are words that have the opposite or nearly the opposite meaning.

> The workers buffed the statue until it shone like a mirror.

Which word is a synonym for *buffed*?

polished	**covered**
tarnished	**dismantled**

Read the answers carefully. Which word means "to make something shine"? The answer is *polish*.

> When she feels morose, she watches funny cartoons to change her mood.

Which word is an antonym of *morose*?

dismal	**agreeable**
happy	**confident**

Think about the sentence. If something funny will change her mood, she must be sad. The answer is *happy*, the antonym of *sad*.

Analogies

This kind of question asks you to find relationships between pairs of words. Analogies usually use *is to* and *as*.

> **green** is to **grass** as _____ is to **sky**

Green is the color of grass. So the answer must be **blue**, the color of the sky.

Roots

A root is a building block for words. Many roots come from ancient languages such as Greek or Latin. Knowing the meaning of a root can often help you figure out the meaning of a word. Note that sometimes the spelling of the root changes.

Root	Language	Meaning	Example
audi	Latin	to hear	audience audible auditorium
bibl	Greek	book	bibliography Bible bibliophile
cred	Latin	to believe	credence creed incredible
dict	Greek	to speak	predict dictionary dictation
finis	Latin	end, limit	finish finally infinite
graph	Greek	to write or draw	autograph biography paragraph
scribe	Latin	to write	describe subscribe prescribe

Prefixes

A prefix is a word part added to the beginning of a base word. A prefix changes the meaning of the base word.

Prefix	Meaning	Base Word	Example
dis-	not, opposite of	like	dislike
mid-	in the middle of	air	midair
mis-	badly, wrongly	behave	misbehave
pre-	before, earlier	cook	precook
re-	again	paint	repaint
sub-	under	freezing	subfreezing
tele-	far away	photo	telephoto
un-	not	happy	unhappy
under-	below, less than	foot	underfoot

Suffixes

A suffix is a word part added to the end of a base word. A suffix changes the meaning of the base word. Sometimes the base word changes spelling when a suffix is added.

Suffix	Meaning	Base Word	Example
-able	able to be, full of	agree	agreeable
-al	relating to	music	musical
-ate	to make	active	activate
-en	to become, to make	light	lighten
-er	person who	teach	teacher
		run	runner
-ful	full of	cheer	cheerful
		beauty	beautiful
-fy	to make	simple	simplify
-ic	like a, relating to	artist	artistic
		athlete	athletic
-ish	like a, resembling	child	childish
-ize	to cause to be	legal	legalize
		apology	apologize
-less	without	hope	hopeless
		penny	penniless
-ly, -ally	in a (certain) way	sad	sadly
		magic	magically
-ship	a state of being	friend	friendship
-ward	in the direction of	east	eastward
-y	like, full of	thirst	thirsty
		fog	foggy

My Vocabulary in Action Dictionary

Categories: *Individual, Visual Learners*

Create your own dictionary of vocabulary words. Take 14 sheets of white paper and one sheet of construction paper and fold them in half. Place the white paper inside the folded construction paper to create a book. Staple the book together on the fold. Label each page of your book with one letter of the alphabet.

At the end of each vocabulary chapter, enter the new words into your dictionary. Include the word, the definition, the part of speech, and a sentence. Each definition should be written in your own words. This will be a good tool to use throughout the year.

Vocabulary Challenge

Category: *Small Group*

Prepare for the game by choosing 15 vocabulary words from the current chapter. Write each word on a separate index card. On the back of the card, write the definition of the word. Place the cards on the floor, with the definition-side down, in three rows of five cards.

Three or four players sit facing the cards. The first player points to a word and gives its definition. If the player gives the correct definition, he or she gets to keep the card. If the player gives the wrong definition, he or she returns the card to the floor.

Players take turns until all the cards are gone. The player with the most cards wins the game.

Vocabulary Quilt

Categories: *Individual or Small Group, Visual Learners*

Find one or two friends to help create a "vocabulary quilt," or create a quilt of your own. Write each vocabulary word from the current chapter in big letters across the top of a separate sheet of construction paper. Illustrate each word, using markers or colored pencils. As you finish, place the pictures in a quilt-like arrangement on a bulletin board. Leave the pictures posted in the room and allow the other students to "visually" learn their vocabulary words.

Toss the Ball

Categories: *Small Group, Kinesthetic Learners*

Find four friends and sit in a circle on the floor. Your group will need a ball and a list of the current chapter's vocabulary words. The first person with the ball says a vocabulary word aloud, then quickly tosses the ball to another person in the group. That person must correctly define the word. If successful, that person says another vocabulary word and tosses the ball to another player. If the word is not defined correctly, the player must leave the circle. The game continues until there is only one player remaining.

© Loyola Press.

For an additional challenge, say a synonym or an antonym for the word instead of a definition.

Synonym Partners

Category: *Large Group*

Write the current chapter's vocabulary words on index cards. Then write a synonym for each word on additional cards. Divide the class into two groups and give the words to one group and the synonyms to the other group.

The object of the game is for each student to find the appropriate synonym partner without speaking or using body language. The partners sit on the floor once they find each other. After all partners are found, each pair tells the class the vocabulary word, its synonym, and the definition.

This game may also be played using an antonym of the vocabulary word instead of a synonym. For a greater challenge, play the game using both a synonym and an antonym without using the vocabulary word.

Catch That Plate

Categories: *Small Group, Kinesthetic Learners*

Write the vocabulary words from the current chapter on slips of paper and place them in a hat. Ask the players to sit in a circle on the floor. Place the hat and a plastic plate in the center. The first player goes to the center of the circle, takes a slip of paper, reads the word, names another player, and spins the plate. The player whose name was called must quickly give a definition for the vocabulary word and then "catch the plate" before it comes to a stop. If successful, that player becomes the new plate spinner. If that player fails to catch the plate in time, the same plate spinner remains.

Vocabulary Egg Shake

Category: *Partners, Kinesthetic Learners*

Find a partner and write the current chapter's vocabulary words on slips of paper. Glue these slips to the inside of each cup section of an egg carton. Place a penny in the egg carton and close the carton. The first partner shakes the carton and then lifts the lid. The second partner must state the correct definition of the vocabulary word on which the penny landed. If successful, he or she must shake the carton. For a variation to this game, state the synonym or antonym for the vocabulary word instead of the definition.

This activity can be used for each new vocabulary chapter by replacing the vocabulary words with new words.

Vocabulary Search

Categories: *Small Group,*
Kinesthetic Learners,
ELL

Form a group of five students. Create alphabet cards from cardboard. Cut out 75 small squares and write one letter of the alphabet on each square. Make two alphabets plus several additional squares for each vowel.

Place the alphabet squares in two piles —with the same letters in each pile—in the middle of the playing area. Designate one person to be the announcer. The remaining four players break into teams of two. The game begins when the announcer says a definition, a synonym, or an antonym of one of the current chapter's vocabulary words. Then each team uses the alphabet cards to try to spell the word to which the announcer is referring. The first team to correctly spell the word receives one point. The team with the most points at the end of the game wins.

Vocabulary Baseball

Category: *Small Group*

Prepare for the game by drawing a baseball diamond on a sheet of paper. Be sure to include three bases and home plate. Write on index cards all of the current chapter's vocabulary words, along with their definitions. Find three friends and divide into two teams. Determine how many innings there will be in the game.

The first team at bat sends its player to home plate. The first player on the other team "pitches" a word to the batter by reading a word. If the batter correctly states the definition, he or she moves to first base. The player continues to move from base to base until he or she crosses home plate or misses the definition. When a player misses, the team gets an out. After three outs, the other team is at bat.

When a player crosses home plate, the team gets one point and the next player bats. The team with the most points at the end of the last inning wins the game.

Vocabulary Fables

Categories: *Individual, Visual Learners*

Reread a popular fairy tale, such as "Cinderella" or "The Three Little Pigs." After you have finished reading the story, write your own version, using at least 10 vocabulary words from the current chapter. Make your new story into a book with illustrated pages and a construction-paper cover. Share your story with your classmates or with another class.

Comic-Strip Vocabulary

Categories: *Individual, Visual Learners*

Prepare for the game by bringing to class some examples of comic strips from newspapers or magazines. Look over the examples for ideas to create your own comic strip. You can either make up new comic-strip characters or use existing characters. Fold a sheet of paper into six equal parts to create six frames. Use at least four of the current chapter's vocabulary words in your story. You should fill each frame with words and pictures. You might display your comic strip or share it with classmates.

Vocabulary Tic-Tac-Toe

Category: *Partners*

Prepare for the game by writing the current chapter's vocabulary words on index cards. Write the definition of the word on the back of the card. You will also need to create five *X* and five *O* cards. Place the vocabulary cards, definition-side down, in a stack. Draw a large tic-tac-toe board on a sheet of paper. Cover each square with a vocabulary card, definition-side down.

Work with a partner. The first player chooses a word and says the definition. If the player is correct, he or she removes the card and replaces it with an *X*. If the player is incorrect, the card goes to the bottom of the vocabulary stack and is replaced with a new card. Then the second player chooses a word and tries to define it. The game continues until a player has successfully made a "tic-tac-toe." This game can be played many times by shuffling the vocabulary cards between rounds.

Word Search Puzzles

Categories: *Partners, Auditory Learners*

Prepare for the game by bringing to class examples of word search puzzles from newspapers, magazines, or books. You will need one sheet of graph paper and a pencil. Use the examples to guide you in creating a word search puzzle that includes some of the vocabulary words from the current chapter. On another sheet of paper, write the definitions of the words you included.

When you have finished your word search puzzle, exchange it with a friend. Take turns reading aloud your definition clues. Your partner must guess the correct vocabulary word and find it in your word search puzzle. Return the word search puzzle to the appropriate owner to check for accuracy.

Tell Me a Story

Category: *Small Group*

Find three partners. You will need two sheets of paper and a pen or pencil. Write all the vocabulary words from the current chapter on one sheet of notebook paper.

One person in the group begins creating a story by writing a sentence or two, using one of the vocabulary words. That person then passes the paper to the next group member. Each player is allowed to use only one vocabulary word each turn. The object of the game is to use all the vocabulary words correctly to form a complete story. The story must make sense, and it must have a beginning, a middle, and an end. Ask someone to check your story for accuracy.

Vocabulary Role-Play

Categories: *Small Group, Kinesthetic Learners, ELL*

Find two partners. Pick 15 vocabulary words from the current chapter. Write each word on a separate small slip of paper. Fold the slips of paper in half and place them in a hat.

Each person selects a word from the hat. When it's your turn, take two minutes to develop a short skit about your word to perform for your partners. In the skit, you must act out your vocabulary word without saying the word. The first person to guess the word correctly draws the next word.

Jeopardy

Categories: *Small Group, Auditory Learners*

Work with three partners. One player starts by giving the definition of a current chapter's vocabulary word. The other three players try to guess the word as quickly as possible. (They do not have to wait for the entire definition.) The first one to guess the word correctly gets to give the next definition. Keep track of who correctly guesses the most words.

Words in Context

Categories: *Partners,*
Technology,
ELL

Work with a partner at a computer. One person enters a vocabulary word from the current chapter. Then the second person enters a sentence using that word correctly. Take turns entering words and sentences. See how many you can complete in 10 minutes. (If you do not have access to a computer, you can write the words and sentences on a sheet of paper.)

Concentration

Categories: *Partners,*
Visual Learners,
ELL

Write eight of the current chapter's vocabulary words on separate index cards. Write the definitions of the words on eight more index cards. Shuffle the cards and place them facedown in a square with four rows of four cards.

Work with a partner. One person turns over two cards. If the definition matches the word, that player keeps the cards. If the definition does not match the word, the player puts the cards facedown in the same places they were before. The other player then turns over two cards. Continue until all the cards have been taken. The partner with the most pairs of cards wins the game.

Index of Words

Here is a list of all the words defined in this book. The number following each word indicates the page on which the word is defined. The Challenge Words are listed in *italics*. The Word Study Words are listed in bold.

abandon, 7
abolish, 27
absolute, 75
abundant, 75
abuse, 17
accommodate, 19
accumulate, 27
acquaint, 41
acquire, 43
acre, 51
actor, 5
adequate, 28
adjust, 61
administer, 13
administrator, 62
admirable, 75
aggressive, 76
alarm, 85
ambition, 7
annoy, 8
annual, 43
antagonize, 57
antiquated, 33
appeal, 17
ascent, 15
ascribe, 83
assent, 15
astonish, 28
atmosphere, 41
authorship, 73
awkward, 53

bacteria, 39
baffle, 57
boast, 76
brothers-in-law, 39
brusque, 91
buff, 85
bureau, 87

camouflage, 13
capital, 15
capitol, 15
caravan, 95
cell, 96

centennial, 13
century, 7
championship, 73
channel, 17
charge, 19
circulation, 27
circumference, 28
clarify, 41
classic, 43
classify, 51
clot, 53
coarse, 61
combat, 8
combustible, 13
comment, 76
common, 85
commotion, 87
compassion, 19
compensation, 96
competition, 95
compile, 33
completion, 96
complicate, 8
compliment, 17
compromise, 62
conclude, 27
confederate, 57
confirm, 101
conflict, 101
conjunction, 28
conscience, 41
consist, 43
contemplate, 51
contraction, 53
convention, 61
corrode, 57
counselor, 5
course, 62
crises, 39
criticize, 75
cultivate, 76

debris, 7
defer, 101
deficient, 33

deflect, 67
deliberately, 87
dependent, 33
describe, 83
destination, 95
deteriorate, 67
devastate, 67
devout, 47
dexterity, 91
diffuse, 67
disassemble, 96
dismal, 13
dissension, 67
distract, 17
dwindle, 47

earnest, 19
encounter, 41
endurance, 23
envious, 23
exceptional, 43
exempt, 48
expenditure, 81
explore, 51
explorer, 5
export, 53

fastidious, 81
forbidding, 61
frame, 75
fraud, 77
friendship, 73
frontier, 85
furnish, 8
furrow, 23

gaudy, 81
genuine, 87
greedily, 96
guarantee, 7
guppy, 17

haggard, 62
hangar, 15
hanger, 15
harmonize, 27

hoarse, 28
homogenize, 41
humility, 81

ideal, 51
illustrate, 53
impenetrable, 48
imperfect, 61
impure, 75
incessant, 92
incident, 77
incidental, 85
inconsiderate, 87
indigo, 95
industry, 97
ineffective, 7
inexpensive, 8
infantry, 17
infection, 19
inflammable, 27
influence, 29
inherent, 19
injection, 43
insane, 51
inscribe, 83
intention, 53
inventor, 5
irrigation, 61
irritate, 63
issue, 75

kerosene, 77
kinship, 73

legend, 85
legislator, 61

magnificent, 87
magnify, 95
manacle, 85
manager, 5
mentality, 7
mercy, 9
midair, 49
midnight, 49
midsize, 49

midterm, 49
midwinter, 49
midyear, 49
migration, 17
mingle, 24
modesty, 24
molecule, 19
mutual, 95

nimble, 41
nourish, 27
novel, 29
nuisance, 43
numb, 51

oblige, 61
observe, 63
orbit, 85
orient, 53
oxen, 39

paltry, 81
parasite, 87
parliament, 95
peerless, 92
perilous, 19
pneumonia, 7
pod, 9

pompous, 92
precipitate, 101
prediction, 27
prescribe, 83
preserve, 29
progress, 41
prompt, 43
proscribe, 83
protein, 51
pulse, 53

ravine, 63
recall, 75
reclaim, 77
recur, 48
reduce, 85
reign, 87
relate, 95
remedy, 97
respectful, 7
revolt, 97
routine, 9

salvation, 17
sanity, 19
satellite, 27
saturate, 33
scandal, 29

scheme, 42
scholarship, 73
security, 43
seep, 53
sentimental, 52
shellac, 61
sinister, 63
solace, 9
sportsmanship, 73
squeamish, 61
steep, 101
sterilize, 63
stern, 75
strive, 77
subfreezing, 93
submarine, 93
submerge, 93
subscribe, 83
subsoil, 93
substandard, 93
subway, 93
suppress, 87
survey, 87
survival, 95

tactics, 97
teeth, 39
telecommunicate, 25

telephone, 25
telephoto, 25
telescope, 25
television, 25
temptation, 7
terrain, 9
testimony, 18
theory, 19
traitor, 27
treaty, 29
triumphant, 42

uncivilized, 43
unexpected, 52

vaccine, 53
vain, 58
vault, 63
vertebra, 75
victorious, 77
vivid, 85

wedge, 95
women, 39
writer, 5

yearn, 97